7 Entrepreneurial Leadership Workouts

7 Entrepreneurial Leadership Workouts

A Guide to Developing Entrepreneurial Leadership in Teams

STEPHANIE JONES AND MARTIN TYNAN

ANTHEM PRESS

Anthem Press
An imprint of Wimbledon Publishing Company
www.anthempress.com

This edition first published in UK and USA 2022
by ANTHEM PRESS
75–76 Blackfriars Road, London SE1 8HA, UK
or PO Box 9779, London SW19 7ZG, UK
and
244 Madison Ave #116, New York, NY 10016, USA

British Library Cataloguing-in-Publication Data
A catalogue record for this book is available from the British Library.

Library of Congress Control Number: 2021948595

ISBN-13: 978-1-83998-184-5 (Hbk)
ISBN-10: 1-83998-184-9 (Hbk)

Cover credit: Powerful business female as company leader with
confidence strength tiny person concept. Businesswoman power with
boss muscles and successful work achievements vector illustration.
Woman leadership. By VectorMine/ Shutterstock.com

This title is also available as an e-book.

Contents

■ ■ ■

Acknowledgements

We would like to thank – collectively – the Maastricht School of Management faculty and staff for making the experience of working on Martin's doctoral degree so pleasant for both of us as supervisor and supervisee. Also the interviewees – entrepreneurial leaders mostly in high-technology businesses in London – who helped Martin so much at this point with their candid and insightful remarks. Then Claudia Huerta – an MBA student at Maastricht School of Management – who took very seriously Martin's ideas for future research on the last page of his DBA thesis and internationalised the project in her MBA thesis paper. In that process we must thank the very many interviewees from all over the planet who contributed to Claudia's research – and therefore also to the present book. We would like to gratefully acknowledge the input of Emilie Morrow, a master's student of entrepreneurship at the University of Cambridge in the United Kingdom, who not only used her exemplary editorial skills to enhance the manuscript but also reflected on the value of the book for herself and fellow students. Also, Roy Arets – a master's student of management, change and consultancy at Maastricht University – helped with sourcing examples of entrepreneurs, marketing ideas and illustrations, and played a key role in focusing on the utility of the book for students as well as practitioners. We are also grateful for the wise comments from our reviewers. Prof. David Bevan used the book as a distraction during the pandemic-enforced lockdown, and Prof. Edward Buckingham as light relief whilst marking the efforts of his students at Monash University in Melbourne, Australia. Our practitioner reviewers, including Tom Jackson of Smart Law and Pardus Bloom (through whom we met Emilie), helped us to see the book through the eyes of a different yet essential audience for us. We would also like to thank Tej, Megan and Courtney at Anthem Press. And last but not least, our long-suffering other halves who have become used to our long hours of absence whilst at the laptop, and especially Martin's children, who remain totally unimpressed.

Introduction

*So, for me personally, the starting point is just thinking about leadership as a skill that can be developed, or **a muscle** that can be developed, and then taking action to do that.*
— An entrepreneurial leader interviewed for this book

Background to This Book: How It Started

The genesis of this book lies in both authors' interests in leadership – and specifically entrepreneurial leadership. One of the authors has a strong grounding in academic research and the other has spent over twenty years working with technology organisations as they have grown and scaled globally. So we have tried to combine theory and practice!

The original material for this book formed part of the doctoral thesis of our practical author, supervised by the academic. Looking at the task of leading the journey from a start-up business to a scaled-up operation, the thesis investigated how and why entrepreneurial leadership practice evolves as the organisation grows, specifically in technology-focused organisations.

The outcome of this doctoral thesis (Maastricht School of Management (MSM), April 2020) was a tentative predictive framework analysing the motivations, roles, behaviours and context of entrepreneurial leadership – and how and why these change and evolve as an organisation moves from start-up to scaled-up. The whole idea was to look for trends and patterns, to give insights to would-be entrepreneurial leaders and their investors. This

1

framework – based on extensive research with entrepreneurial leaders across Europe, North America and South America, and supported by interviews from a selection of worldwide locations (including India, China and the Middle East, researched by MSM MBA student Claudia Huerta, September 2020) – has been further developed and honed to focus on seven key 'workouts' which entrepreneurial leadership teams need 'to go for and train for' as they work and strive to take their nascent start-ups to more scaled-up operations.

There are obviously many factors involved in this process of a business moving from this embryonic stage to a mature operation – beyond the immediate issue of leadership: the product or service itself, the nature of the market opportunity for the product or service, the timing of market entry, the funding of the organisation and so on. Additionally, a key part of this is the capability and ability of the organisation through its people – not just the founding leadership team, but the employees in the company – to also scale and grow. It could be argued that one of the most important factors in the scaling and growing process is the competence and motivation of the individuals within the organisation. Yet, this issue of human capital, so often identified as *the* key component of driving organisational growth, does not even have a name on the company balance sheet, and if it does, it is lumped under 'intangibles'!

As mentioned above, one of the key audiences for the present study has been identified as the investors-in-start-ups community – and increasingly they are showing more interest in the 'leadership' element which drives the creation (or in some cases the destruction) of these 'intangible' elements of a company's value. At the same time, there also appears to be a lack of confidence in the ability of investors to assess leadership capability, yet anecdotal research shows that when making investment decisions, investors place around a 30–50 per cent weighting of that investment decision on the 'leadership strength' of an organisation, however that is defined.

Financial measures (revenue growth, customer numbers, amount of dollars in market opportunity, etc.) on how to predict the likely success of a company have always existed in analysing company value. These measures can be used by the current and potential stakeholders in a start-up organisation as a way of assessing the likely future success of this business from start-up to scaled-up mode.

However, investors and stakeholders are showing increased interest in identifying a method to measure the more 'intangible' aspects of a company's potential growth. A significant part of these intangibles includes current and future leadership capability and competence. This is of particular interest to investors, when more and more of the intangible value of an organisation, and the ability to grow from a start-up to a scale-up organisation, is undoubtedly related to the success or failure of the founding leadership team.

The purpose of this book has therefore been to focus on a specific aspect of these 'intangibles' – the capability, competence and skill set of the entrepreneurial leadership team. What is the collective leadership 'muscle' needed to grow, develop and scale the organisation? Which particular 'muscles', and how can they be identified, developed and exercised? And in the process of doing so, the focus of the present study is to provide ideas, strategies and tactics to offer tangible support to entrepreneurial leaders/founders, investors, employees and other stakeholders in the business. The objective here is to pinpoint some of the key capabilities, competencies and skill sets of entrepreneurial leadership which can have a direct impact on enabling the business to grow, develop and scale up to achieve its potential and sustainable future.

Furthermore, having identified these capabilities, competencies and skill sets – the 'organisational muscle' as we have described it – this book then provides a series of 'workouts' to help the leadership teams in the organisation to grow and develop this muscle power. In doing so, they will enable the entrepreneurial leadership team to grow, develop and scale up the organisation, in a much more systematic, measurable and specific way – a bit more like the financial measures!

Why Does This Matter?

Although many observers argue that start-up organisations are important for creating job opportunities, it is the 'scaled up' organisations that actually make more career opportunities on a larger and sustained scale and drive economic growth within countries, especially for the future. Particularly high-growth, sustainably scaled-up businesses are widely seen as supporting economic resilience, especially in challenging times – now reaching a crescendo as this book goes to press (October 2021). The current need for economic recovery, let alone growth, is more desperate than ever. The takeaway here is that although there is no issue with the number of start-ups right now – there are very many – the challenge is how to get some of these companies to scale up? To not just survive, but thrive? Especially at a time when many new innovative start-ups have emerged in the totally volatile, uncertain, complex, ambiguous (VUCA) era of the early 2020s – but how many will last?

For every Amazon, Facebook, Netflix and Google there are literally thousands of small start-ups trying to 'scale-up' to become the next Slack, Zoom or Uber. Less than 1 per cent of these start-ups will make it to the big time. For would-be entrepreneurs, for employees working in a start-up, for an investor – how to tell if the business-in-the-back-bedroom will ever see its name in lights? Does the entrepreneurial team in question have the required 'muscle power' to succeed? Of the huge array of start-ups founded each year, how do investors increase their chances of backing the one in a thousand that will become a scaled-up company? How can an investor talent-spot entrepreneurial muscle power? Many would-be founders have a view to setting up new business ventures, spurred on by opportunities presented by the changing world. Given the current environment we are experiencing, this will no doubt spur on new start-ups being founded to address new challenges or opportunities in the market or to address current challenges or opportunities in a different way. It can easily be argued that the rate of start-ups during the totally unpredictable world of the 2020s continues to increase day by day. Given that this uncertainty and need for adaptation, and the response of entrepreneurial leaders to this, are such key drivers of organisational scale-up success, how can stakeholders in an organisation increase and work on the 'organisational muscle' that will improve the chances of their start-up organisation succeeding to scale up where other scale-ups will disappear?

Here, we argue that it all depends on whether these founders have this special *entrepreneurial leadership muscle* – or if they can see it and nurture it in others. As entrepreneurs, how can these founders identify, develop, build and use this necessary 'muscle' to make things happen in a sustainable way? As investors, what are the readable signs of 'muscle power' amongst the entrepreneurial leaders passing the radar screens? How can they screen in and screen out?

The Start-Up Situation: The Anatomy of the Entrepreneurial Leader

At its simplest level, there are two types of entrepreneurs: those who are necessity-driven and those who are opportunistically driven. For the purposes of this book, we will differentiate between the two, focusing on the latter.

Necessity-driven entrepreneurs are those who have no choice or limited choices in how to make a living. These are often seen (but not exclusively) in countries with less mature economies and economies that do not provide a decent social security safety net. A good example of this might be street hawkers or traders in less developed countries. They are not always sole traders/entrepreneurs/businesspeople out of choice – often (but not exclusively) it is out of necessity. They work at their job because they need to.

Opportunistically driven entrepreneurs are often those who by choice or design decide to set up their own business – and thus establishing their organisation or joining a recently established organisation as a leader at a relatively early stage in its life cycle – and they become entrepreneurial leaders. They typically have other opportunities/choices open to them and are making a conscious choice to become opportunity-driven entrepreneurs.

For the purposes of this book, we are focusing on those who are in the opportunistic bucket. Given that they usually have different options about their career choice, or how they earn a living, the *motivation* of entrepreneurial leaders in their choice is an important point as we look to organisations to further develop and grow their 'muscle'. Entrepreneurial leaders must possess this motivation to want to grow and develop. This has been our starting point, and this must be where you – our readers – are currently at!

How the Book Is Organised and How the Book Can Be Used

The book is organised into seven organisational muscle 'workouts' – which the authors have identified as key for the entrepreneurial leadership team to grow and develop, in order that the organisation can grow and develop in parallel. As previously discussed, the identification of these 'muscles' is based on the doctoral research thesis of one of the authors (Martin Tynan), which involved extensive conversations with successful entrepreneurial leaders in Europe, the Americas and beyond, including Asia. As the book is based on this research, we thought it appropriate to include the 'voices' and experiences of these entrepreneurial leaders in each chapter. Through these 'voices' the reader can hear an authentic articulation of the everyday practical issues faced by entrepreneurial leaders, and our hope is that this echoes through the workouts and that these shared ideas and comments will resonate with readers (current entrepreneurial leaders, soon-to-be entrepreneurial leaders, would-be investors or stakeholders in a start-up organisation, or a student studying entrepreneurial leadership). The 'voices' are therefore included to bring the workouts to life and encourage and enable their practical application in the modern business and management world.

Each chapter comprises three parts:

- Part 1, where the 'organisational muscle' to be developed is discussed.
- Part 2, where we hear the unfiltered, authentic voices of the entrepreneurial leaders and their practical, candid reflections.
- Part 3, where we ask a series of questions to be discussed/ answered by the organisation, which then leads into a series of

specific workouts that the organisational leadership team can experience.

High-Level Overview of Each of the Workouts

Here, we give a very high-level overview of each specific muscle and workout to be developed before moving into the specific discussion and workout of the muscles themselves in the rest of the chapters.

Workout 1: Letting Go of Autonomy – from Founder-Led to Team Leadership – and Beyond

This chapter focuses on the organisational need to move from founder-led leadership (a desire to have autonomy and control over the organisation) to adapting to a more shared and agile leadership style. To scale up the organisation, the founding team needs to devolve more and more of the organisational decisions into the broader organisational context. There is inherent risk in doing this. Does the business have the capability to absorb this extra decision-making responsibility? Does it have the muscle power already? If not, how can it be built? Developing the organisational muscle for the current leadership to adapt a more agile leadership style – coupled with the organisational capability to absorb and perform in this changing context – is a key component of this aspect of organisational development.

WORKOUT TO BUILD ADAPTABILITY, AGILITY, DELEGATION, WIDER PARTICIPATION IN DECISION-MAKING, TAKING ON MORE RESPONSIBILITY THROUGHOUT

Workout 2: Anticipating Future Problems – from Solving One at a Time to Coping with Many – from the Here-and-Now to the Future

Typical organisations founded today are often addressing a defined business need or identified business problem to be solved. Start-up organisations thrive on and celebrate organisational 'heroes' who can solve problems and then move on to solving the next challenge. This tends to be reactive rather than pro-active. This reactive and responsive capability is an important organisational muscle to have at the early stage of the start-up journey. It can be particularly prevalent in technology-focused organisations, where a 'test and learn' mantra is common. Releasing products with potentially known or unknown issues is a trade-off for getting the product or service to market as quickly as possible. However, as the organisation grows and scales, this muscle can be overused and overstretched. Not all employees thrive on solving the reactive problem, and customers that were forgiving of known problems with service at the start (early adopters) can now be less forgiving. A significant amount of organisational energy and resources can be used up addressing reactive problems.

An inflection point comes when organisations need to move to anticipating and solving future potential organisational problems upfront rather than reactively and retroactively addressing the challenge. Again, this is not a sudden shift in organisational momentum; however, it is an organisational muscle that needs to be developed. Often, this is an organisational capability that does not necessarily exist within the current framework of the organi-sation and most likely needs to be acquired and augmented from external sources.

WORKOUT *TO LET GO OF REACTIVENESS; TO SHIFT DIREC-TION FROM RESPONDING TO CREATING; TO BUILD PROAC-TIVITY, INITIATIVE, OPENNESS TO NEW IDEAS; TO CHALLENGE THE STATUS QUO*

Workout 3: Changing Focus – from Being Customer-Focused to Problem-Solving 360° for the Customer – from Looking Outside (at Customers and Opportunities) to Looking Inside (Managing the Business Internally)

Companies that are business to consumer (b2c) rather than business to business (b2b) obsess about the customer. Having a strong customer-focus mentality is key to an organisation gaining the initial market momentum. This is often linked to problem-solving as early adopters of a product or service are actively encouraged to give feedback on the product or service. This feedback loop with the customer allows the organisation to refine/review their product offering to the user, building loyalty and commitment. By actively involving the end consumer, these companies and teams have a strong customer focus to build the product that the customers desire and want – but this might occur at the expense of building internal capacity.

Again, an inflection point occurs when the organisation scales up and the customer feedback and input grow, and the business must address and solve the wishes and desires of an increasing number of customers. Additionally, what is often seen is that the external customer-interface muscle is rather well developed in the organisation, but the internal organisational muscle or capability to deliver on the customer's needs, for the sustainable long term, is rather less evident. This is akin to a swimmer focusing more on one arm for their swimming stroke and less on the other arm. They can still effectively swim from one end of the pool to the other, but not as efficiently or effectively as if they focused on both arms at the same time.

Beginning the process of building the right internal systematic organisation capability (systems, processes, procedures) to deliver the product or service to the customer is an important realignment that often needs to occur. Again, the organisational muscle used to focus on the customer externally cannot easily adapt to the need to balance this with organisational capability to deliver for the customer. This is often seen in the tensions and trade-offs between the organisational sales team (give the customer what they want to drive revenue) with the internal product or service team who are tasked with building, developing or refining the product (at what cost do we deliver the product?)

WORKOUT *TO WIDEN FOCUS, CHANGE DIRECTION, CHANGE MOTIVATION SOURCES, CHANGE OBSESSIONS; TO MANAGE ORGANISATIONAL CAPABILITY TO RESPOND; TO BUILD TEAMWORK; TO DEVELOP RESOURCES AND NOT JUST USE THEM*

Workout 4: Allowing for Role Evolution – from Lack of Role Clarity to Role Definition

Often at the start of an organisation's journey, the relatively small number of employees in the organisation wear multiple hats. Additionally, employees often have more discretion over what they would like to do in the organisation rather than focusing on what needs to be done in the organisation. Moreover, the founding leadership team often has ill-defined roles. They just have a go at everything.

As the organisation grows and scales from a role-evolution perspective, two things begin to occur. At the organisational leadership level, roles need to become more specialist and less generalised. The founding leader cannot be the chief strategy officer as well as the chief finance officer and chief customer officer at the same time. The organisation needs to identify the organisational capability and muscle that each of the founding leaders brings to the organisation and more clearly define their roles. Because these are also the founders in the organisation, the Board can play an important part in this process. The Board (and investors) can have delicate organisational conversations that steer founding leaders towards the more defined roles they will have in the organisation as it develops.

Also, often the founding leaders might not have the broad experience required for some specialist roles such as the chief finance officer – this can be an organisational muscle that the organisation does not have time for and lacks the appetite to develop – and thus they may need to augment the senior team at this stage. From an employee perspective, this can also impact the roles that employees perform and the tasks they undertake, which need to be more clearly defined with the more complex organisational topography and the system growth that is happening in the organisation. This 'role definition' muscle is often one of the hardest to identify and execute.

WORKOUT *TO GAIN CLARITY, DEFINITION, TASK ORIENTATION, CHANGE GOALS; TO DEFINE ORGANISATIONAL CAPABILITY NEEDED FOR THE FUTURE; TO BUILD MORE DIRECTED TEAMS; TO NAVIGATE COMPLEXITY*

Workout 5: Coping with Risk – from One Single Point of Failure to Juggling Several Products, Processes and People Issues – Understanding Systemic Risk

Managing and coping with organisational risk is an inherent part of a business as it starts up and moves to scale-up mode. Risks always exist – for example, the risk of making decision A coupled with the risk of *not* making decision A. At either end of the spectrum, the nature of the risk differs. At the early stage of the start-up, there is one overriding risk – the concern that the organisation will fail or will fail to scale up beyond the start. There are several other overriding risks, which give rise to a small number of key decisions that need to be undertaken by a small number of people. As the organisation grows, the number of risks increases but the overriding risks tend to subside; however, these risks are then distributed amongst a larger number of people (which can have its own pros and cons).

WORKOUT TO COPE WITH RISK, TAKE CHANCES, WEIGH UP PROS AND CONS BUT NOT BE SUCKED INTO THE BLACK HOLE OF ENDLESS ANALYSIS; TO REALISE WHAT HAPPENS IF NOTHING HAPPENS; TO SEE THE IMPACT ON THE BIG PICTURE; TO SEE IMPLICATIONS FURTHER DOWN THE LINE; TO MINIMISE RISK

Workout 6: Managing Culture Change – Understanding Person–Culture Fit from an Additive Start-Up to Matching the Values of a Sustainable Business

In growing a company from a start-up venture to a more mature scaled-up organisation, culture plays an important part in 'how we do things around here'. Scaling an organisation involves scaling a mindset, a specific approach about how an organisation identifies customer problems, delivers products/services to meet customer needs and balances internal and external resources and requirements. Some start-ups consciously focus on setting the right culture in their organisation, and as they hire new people they look to see if these new employees 'fit' the culture of the business. Other organisations tend to put a less rigorous framework on the culture, leaving it to grow in a less deliberate way (which will happen anyway). Regardless of which approach is taken, an organisational culture emerges from the start-up organisation – either consciously or unconsciously. This can be role modelled by leaders and key employees or emerge in aspects of how decisions are made. As the organisation grows, the current 'culture' begins to evolve and change in a greater or lesser degree as each new employee comes on board. As the organisation develops and grows its organisational capability and muscle (through each new employee), the employee brings not just their talent and capability but also their way of doing things. Each new employee either 'fits' into the culture of the organisation – how they tend to do things is how the company tends to want them to do things – or comes on board and is more 'additive' to the culture – though they may generally do things the way the organisation does things, some aspects of how they do things might differ. If the employee is a senior member or a leader in the organisation, this 'new way of doing things' can become a part of 'how we do things around here', and the culture begins to evolve and change.

Likewise, the new person hired could be consciously brought into the organisation to develop new cultural 'muscle' – bring new ideas/fresh ways of doing things. Thus, whether it is conscious or unconscious, the organisation's culture begins to evolve and adapt as each new employee joins the organisation. The challenge for the company is to define how much they want the culture to be flexible and be additive to new ways of doing things or how much rigour the current leadership team puts on the current culture. Again, there is no one way of doing this; it involves being consciously aware that whether or not an organisation decides to do something about the evolving culture, it will develop by itself. Like a child going from adolescence to adulthood, an organisation that wants to scale up and grow will go on a similar journey. There are aspects of the development that you can influence and control, but there are also aspects of this that you have less control over.

***WORKOUT** TO IDENTIFY CULTURAL NORMS; TO BUILD THE IDENTIFIED CULTURE; TO BE CONSTRUCTIVE; TO WORK ON HOW THINGS WORK; TO ABSORB NEW CULTURES, NOT TO REJECT BUT TO CO-OPERATE; TO INTEGRATE*

Workout 7: Building a Growth Mindset – from Start-Up to Sustainable Growth

The boxer-cum-philosopher Mike Tyson is well known for his famous saying: 'Everyone has a plan till they get a punch in the face.' Similarly, start-up organisations may have a theory or vision of how their product or service will work in the marketplace. They could approach the market with a fully baked product/service, having done extensive market research, or they might approach the market with a beta or test product that they will use to gain practical insight and feedback from customers in the market. Customer feedback can be negative – customers refuse to buy their product or, when they do buy it, they give terrible feedback on the product or service, either directly to the company or through review listings and websites. Conversely, feedback can be positive – consumers love and adopt the new product/service and give it great feedback.

The company can know the actual consumer reaction to their start-up company only by launching their product or service into the market. Regardless of which reaction the product or service receives, being open to the feedback from employees, stakeholders and customers is an important part of the organisational muscle to develop – and often one of the hardest. As the marketplace throws metaphorical punches at your start-up product and service, the organisation needs to develop the capability and the muscle to absorb the punches, while also reacting and adapting to the external landscape in which they are operating.

WORKOUT *TO BE OPEN TO FEEDBACK; TO BE RECEPTIVE BUT RESILIENT; TO BE EXPERIMENTAL; TO BE ADVENTUROUS; TO TAKE FEEDBACK POSITIVELY AND CONSTRUCTIVELY; TO ABSORB AND USE POSITIVE AND NEGATIVE CRITICISM; TO BE FOCUSED ON LONG-TERM GROWTH*

Now that we have outlined the workouts, let us begin the journey of exploring how to develop your own organisation's entrepreneurial leadership muscle!

1

Workout 1: Letting Go of Autonomy – from Founder-Led to Team Leadership – and Beyond

- Ceding personal/individual autonomy to the leadership team as a whole
- Then letting go of control and autonomy from that initial leadership team into the wider organisation to enable it to grow
- Followed by delegating and devolving decision-making and responsibility further down the hierarchy to develop empowerment in the organisation

Part 1: Discussion of the Organisational Muscle to Be Developed

Imagine you want to join a rugby team or rowing team or another team-based sports group. Being obsessed with autonomy and individually wanting to go it alone, with total control and responsibility for yourself, is just not going to work. All the members of the team need to build up their individual muscle power to match the performance of the whole team so that the team can achieve its chosen objectives. Then – we need to think of the wider club with the team members on the benches – they need to be empowered and involved too. And even the management, coaches, trainers and the fans. Everyone needs and wants to be included and not left out. Letting go of personal autonomy is just the start.

For the founders of start-up companies, this sports team could be an image or metaphor for one of *the first major challenges* they face as leaders, as their embryonic business grows and they let go – in other words, how they move from having full control and autonomy over the organisation to building the entrepreneurial team muscle – ensuring that they delegate and devolve tasks and responsibilities more into the start-up for it to grow and develop and eventually scale up. It's all about teamwork.

As discussed in the introduction, a major motivational driver for entrepreneurial leaders to establish their new organisation in the first place – or join the business before it has really scaled up – is this desire for *autonomy* in the work that they do.

This desire by entrepreneurial leaders for autonomy can be driven by a need for *control* and *responsibility*. It can be a reaction to their experiences before. It's something they want.

Why? Entrepreneurial leaders who have founded their own companies tend to come broadly from three work backgrounds:

- They have worked in larger organisations;
- They have worked in other similar, smaller start up organisations before; or
- They have no experience working in an organisation with other people at all.

In each of the three ways, they may be used to autonomy, control and responsibility, and want to keep it, either consciously or unconsciously. Each of these three backgrounds, while different, has an important influence on the level of control and autonomy that exists and may be desired for the founder and/or among the founders and leaders in the organisation at the early stage.

For the founding leaders who have worked in larger organisations, often the background to setting up their own company is because they have experienced personal lack of control and lack of autonomy in these large corporates – and they don't like it. One of the drivers of setting up their own venture can be in response to their negative experiences in a larger, well-established business.

For entrepreneurial leaders who have worked in other similar, smaller start-ups, they would have experienced similar levels of control and autonomy previously, so this level of control and autonomy in what they do is something they are used to and enjoy. It could be behind the reason they started the new business in the first place.

For those founding leaders with no previous organisational background, they likely have no other experience than being in control and being autonomous in how they do their work. They may have been freelancers or one-person bands and that's all they know.

Ultimately, they want control over their own destiny – hence the reason for founding the start-up venture, as an extension of themselves.

As with any start-up, at the early stages there are very few employees – often just the founding team – so this small team exerts a large level of control and autonomy over the general direction and focus of the nascent organisation.

Even when a couple or more people join the venture, there is a still a relatively small number of people involved, so leadership control over and by this small group is quite strong – and it is relatively easy and straightforward for the leadership team to exert significant control.

Centralised control at this early stage tends to be a positive as it provides clear direction and focus and supports the new venture in allocating relatively scarce resources as it looks to establish itself in the market with its product or service.

This exertion of control can be seen in how decisions are made, what the product or service features will look like, and the nature of the go-to-market strategy.

All of these decisions are made initially by a small group of people who have founded the organisation.

However, in the background is the thought of the rugby or rowing team – and the need to build the collective muscle to work together to win, and to have an overall fit body performing at a high level and leading the business.

So, already built into the new venture is *the second major entrepreneurial leadership fitness challenge* it will face. They let go of some individual autonomy, but from the outset, tension and strain are in-built in the founding leadership team. Why?

Challenge 1: I Am Not Alone!

Entrepreneurial leadership teams are, by definition, operating as a collective force. The popular myth of the lone founder battling the odds by themselves is purely that – a myth! Often, particularly in successful start-ups from scratch, the venture is a collective enterprise – with several founders and early leaders – not just one sole founding leader.

This tension is automatic and inevitable in the founding leadership team, as the individuals involved battle for autonomy and their place in the new entity. Some have a need to control their destinies – that's why they chose the start-up route – but soon realise that this must be tempered with the messy collective leadership process of working, agreeing, deciding and allocating resources with others. However, the trade-offs involved here can create a lot of tension at the early stages. Entrepreneurial leaders must find and develop their collective and collaborative muscle. If they have only asserted their autonomy, control and responsibility muscles, they have a few workouts ahead of them to help play their part to get the venture on the right track. A stark reality hits the founding leaders: 'To scale and grow my start-up business, I need to work with others. It can't just be me. Entrepreneurial leadership is a team sport.'

Challenge 2: To Be Successful, I Need More People!

Stark reality #2 hits. To scale and grow the company, the founding team needs to hire more people into the business! As the organisation grows, it must hire more employees to support expansion and growth. This can be twofold: bringing in new employees to work in existing roles or to work in newly created roles which are now needed during scale-up.

This expansion of the employee base in the organisation can also include the recruitment of new leaders. As there are more and more tasks to be performed and more and more decisions to be made, the organisational requirement often dictates the need to delegate and cede more of the control to other employees and other leaders in the business.

This theme will be explored more in future workouts in this book. And as we saw in the introduction and as we touch upon below, hiring more people is a test – and it's highly revealing. The founding team may be hesitant and conservative, and may under-hire. The people they bring in may struggle to rise to the challenge of their tasks. Or they might hire for today – the current tasks – and soon the new people might be out of their depth. Relatively few founding teams have the courage to bring in talent who are highly qualified and able to help the new business to reach a new level – quickly.

Part 2: Experiences of Entrepreneurial Leaders – Letting Go of Autonomy

The entrepreneurial leaders who were interviewed as part of our rese arch identified autonomy as a big driver or motivator to founding or establishing their own start-up – but they then realised they had to let go and appreciate the collective leadership team. They recognised the need to delegate and to bring more empowerment to all the people in the developing organisation, and that this is an important organisational muscle to develop – the ability to delegate tasks and devolve decision-making deeper and wider into the business.

This also requires an ability to reflect on the entrepreneurial leadership strengths and weaknesses and where additional organisational muscle might need to be brought in. How to scale the team and continually develop the overall organisational capability, skill and muscle to execute the company's roadmap and plan?

It is not enough just to hire people into the organisation – there's a need to empower them, cede control and responsibility to them, for both established tasks and new decision-making needs.

Autonomy

The start-up entrepreneurs whom we interviewed in our research seem to align on a similar starting point. They wanted autonomy, they wanted to be in control of how, when and what they worked on.

Here are some of the voices of the entrepreneurial leaders as they reflected on their own experiences:

> For me, the push to be an entrepreneur was a greater sense of autonomy. I've worked in corporates. I've been working for 20 years, and 10 were in the corporate world, and 10 in start-ups, and only the last 4 years were in a company that I've owned or that I've run by myself. I just wanted to be the *master of my own destiny*.
>
> I've always described the need to be an entrepreneur as less of a motivation, and more of a sort of lack of a choice. There wasn't a sense of 'Shall I work for [Company X], or shall I do my own business?' There was *no choice*.
>
> You're in control of your own destiny. That's the simple answer. If you work for someone else, you're always either a number or you are just not in control. For me, it's very important for to be *in control* of my life and my goals. That's why the only way to achieve that is finding and starting a business.
>
> For me it's about the kind of people you want to spend your time with. I'm always surprised when people go to work doing a job, in a company, with people – that *they don't like*. Why keep doing something you don't like? What's the point?
>
> It is not possible to have the whole control of the business as a start-up; it is always a team effort, you always hear about the lead entrepreneur, but *there is always a team of people* working behind the business. I have always relied on others; we need each other to grow the business.

Entrepreneurial Leadership Is a Collective Process!

As discussed earlier in the chapter, the myth of the lone entre-preneur battling individually is somewhat at odds with the real-life experiences of entrepreneurial leaders. Successfully taking an organisation from start-up to scale-up is a *collective experience*. Some entrepreneurs wanted to do this from their first start-up. For other entrepreneurial leaders, it was part of the learning process, trying to do something by themselves. When it was not successful, they realised from their failures that success is a collective process.

Having other voices in the room, having other partners with you on the journey (while sometimes challenging) was an important part of the process.

> You'll have to make individual decisions, but at some point and on most issues, you realise you need a co-founder, because then it's a *collective* decision. So you've got two brains instead of one. And especially in start-ups you need people you can go to for bigger strategic decisions and how to take the first step.
>
> Keeping those collective relationships is key. I was asked about my biggest achievement. I said, 'I'm still with my key partner that I started the company with.' We've come from absolutely nothing to now having a little bit of a business, *together.*
>
> There's always this thing about famous celebrity *lone entrepreneurs* who built companies, but they didn't do it single-handedly, nobody does. That's the one thing about the leaders who are coming up; they recognise that they're going to *need people* to build a fantastic company. They're *not going to do it themselves.*
>
> I think in start-ups you're likely to have a lot of people who are entrepreneurial because you need them to be. As you're growing and scaling, you need lots of people who've got that mindset of, 'Let's think about this *differently.* Let's quickly give this a go.'
>
> There are four of us. I wouldn't be able to start anything by myself. I've tried in the past. I was trying to start a number of businesses since the age of 15.
>
> You need to have business partners, simply for the fact that you need to have business partners who are *different.* If you have all the same characteristics in the room, then it's not going to go anywhere.
>
> You need a bunch of people where most of the time you're going to *disagree.* And then come to the best decision. It's good to have people who, if you've been down, may just drag you up. If they fall down, you drag them up. You have that camaraderie. Feeling like you can do *something together.*

Delegation Is Key!

Even if you start the organisation with a number of other leaders, the entrepreneurial leaders we spoke to in our research soon learned that they needed to delegate more tasks and responsibilities to other people in the organisation. They could not do it all themselves.

Often, this involved hiring more employees into the organisation – which is, again, a key organisational muscle to develop.

> It was an incredibly stressful period because I wasn't really set up. I was *almost doing everything by myself* and I found it hard to ask people to do things because I wasn't paying them much … but when the company started to get busy and too much had to happen, then I had to *change*.
>
> I think it is okay *not to be strong in everything*. I think you need to be consistent, helping your people to eventually accept their strengths and how they cover the weaknesses.
>
> In the past I've brought in more experienced people to help run the company, the Board, and the finance side. The trouble is, as a person I'm capable of doing lots of things, and invariably there's some things I do that'll take me longer or I can get bogged down in – and I think the challenge there is trying to *delegate* around myself.
>
> In leadership training in the military you are taught a structure of how to be a leader because of how you give instruction, *how you delegate individual tasks* to different elements of the team.
>
> Success for me in my role is the *positive evolution* of my team and that we *bring in new talent* for the next phase of our growth.
>
> I hired a consultant in agreement with my associate, *because we desperately needed to free up our time*, there were too many people not working effectively.

Not Just Giving Employees Tasks but Trusting Them to Do the Tasks

However, it is not enough just to bring employees into the organisation. As entrepreneurial leaders, you need to empower these new employees to do their jobs. You have to trust that fact that you are hiring smart people into your organisation – they must be additive to your business and to your culture – so you need to trust them, listen to them and empower them.

> I've seen really successful start-up leaders who bring in trustworthy, fantastic people and then let them get on with it. Bring advisors that they *trust*. People who will tell them if something is wrong, or they're doing something wrong, and they *listen* to them.
>
> We'd hired people, we'd *empowered* them, and we're letting them get on with it. But there may be stories I'm totally unaware of, about junior people making bad decisions, because we hadn't

given them the *infrastructure or help*, to help them make better
choices. It took a while to get it right.

At the beginning control was very important for me, but I realized
that every company has a life and it must be able to go on
even without me; I understood this pretty soon thanks to the
mentors I have had. I could not keep track of every detail, *I
needed people to support me*, people who, though similar to me,
could be independent. So developing people is so important,
especially in the areas where they are stronger than I am.

Letting Go Is Hard – Really Hard!

However, letting go is not an easy process for most entrepreneurial
leadership individuals and teams. There is this tension and angst
in ceding control to other people in the organisation. Some
entrepreneurial leaders have a blind spot around this – sometimes, it takes a while for them to become aware of this tendency;
it can be subconscious.

I wouldn't say I am as involved as I used to be when we started,
but I am still looking over things that I would like to delegate.
But we just started a new phase, hiring a lot of new people that
still need to be completely trained to take complete charge
over some of these responsibilities. I don't like bothering with
the administrative and operational details; I would rather just
get involved head-on with the projects, but *for me to be completely
free of all responsibility is still going to take a while.*

Time has taught me about this the hard way. I felt like I had to
deal with every detail of the company, *it took valuable time away
from me*. So once I had the opportunity to start delegating,
I had no problem; I realized I needed to do it.

Yes, my need for autonomy and control changed, because
when we grew I had new responsibilities and had to *delegate*.
There comes a time where it is impossible to be in charge of
everything. But my autonomy is really important, in the sense
that I'm in charge of my own agenda and I want to keep it that
way. *Which is also hard to manage because people want a piece of you.*

I personally struggled with letting go of the processes and
trusting people, but I was forced to – *I couldn't help my business
grow if I kept holding onto everything*. I have learned during the
last couple of years how to build my relationships with my
collaborators and employees so that they can take charge of
some responsibilities.

Control was really important for me; it had to be if I wanted my vision of the company to succeed. It was a complete change from what it used to be, but *when I can trust someone working for me*, I am more than happy to let go and give them control.

After five years I feel like I am *less controlling*, but it is still really important to me doing my own thing.

I make sure that we meet the revenues, otherwise *I still like having my freedom of working* – however I see fit. I am pretty hands-off with the work of my staff. We touch base for the important things, otherwise I don't think it's necessary to give them very close follow-up.

I like my autonomy, but I don't have so much anymore, and regarding control I do it less now than when I started, and I don't look for control in an active way. With the company growing *I can't afford to control so much*, as I have more responsibilities to attend to.

Successful Leadership – Your Company Runs Itself!

For some entrepreneurial leaders, the definition of successfully taking an organisation from start-up to scale-up is that the business can eventually run itself. They create an environment and a context, where they have hired talented people, empowered them, trusted them – and it is these people who can take the organisation to the next level.

I don't really think about controlling my businesses – my start-ups are so hit-and-miss I don't really feel I need to control them – if someone comes in to help then that gives me more freedom to do other things and it might be more likely to succeed. I am often busy with my different businesses, so *I'm quite happy if anyone wants to help me* do four or five of them.

I believe the aim should be to create a business that *can run without you*. Personally I'm happy with delegating, but I still like being involved because I really care about my business. I know I must let go but I don't think I have people who care as much about my company as I do. I am starting to delegate more and I'm trying to find the right talent or coaching the people so that I can completely let go of some responsibilities.

For me autonomy is important, but I want my *business to be sustainable and autonomous*, I want it to run by itself. That way I have more time to focus on other things.

In this section of the chapter, we have heard the real-life experiences and voices of entrepreneurial leaders as they reflected on the challenges of developing the organisation muscle to delegate responsibility and ceding aspects of control of the organisation to other people within the organisation. This can be an incredibly challenging muscle for the organisation and for the entrepreneurial leadership team to develop; however, as the experiences of those who have successfully started and scaled up their organisations show, this is a vital muscle to develop to enable the organisation to grow and prosper. In the next section of the chapter, we will provide a framework in which organisations can identify the current state of the organisational muscle and provide a series of exercises or workouts that the organisation can perform in order to further develop this key organisational muscle.

Part 3: Organisational Muscle Workout Practice – Moving from the Current State to the Future State

- Understand the current and necessary future state of this organisational muscle.
- Through this then identify the organisational muscle to be developed.
- Put in place a 'workout' plan to develop the muscle – with milestones, targets and regular check-ins on whether the muscle is being developed – or not.

In this workout there is a need to build entrepreneurial leadership muscle throughout the organisation – delegating and devolving more decision-making and responsibility throughout the team, as part of the process of letting go. The letting go comes first – as an essential prerequisite to building the muscle in everyone else.

The first stage of the process is an honest assessment of where the organisation is today. Using these seven key questions, can you assess the state of the current organisational muscle?

1. Are you all alone with the business, and just supported by junior staff? Scaling an organisation is a collective process.

Do you have leadership partners you can trust on the journey ahead? If not, you need to hire some!

2. If you currently have a leadership team in place, do you trust that you have the *right mix of skills/capabilities/experience* on your leadership team for the journey ahead? The right mix of operational, marketing, revenue-generating, technology, back-office leadership skills? If not, can some of the leadership team develop this capability, or do you need to bring someone in with this capability already developed? Do you need to move beyond the original entrepreneurial leadership team?

3. When do you need this new leadership skill set in place? Do you need to hire additional complementary leadership muscle to grow the organisation – now? Three months later? Twelve months later? You need to think about it.

4. Are you willing and comfortable as a leadership team to cede control and responsibility to a new person? This will be key to both individual and organisational successes. What level of control and responsibility are you willing to cede and devolve?

5. Can you currently delegate tasks and responsibilities to more junior members of staff? If not, is it their capability and experience that is the concern, or is it your leadership style of not wanting to let go getting in the way?

6. Do you micromanage tasks that you should trust other people to do in the company? Or are you obsessed as a leadership team with small tasks that could be delegated to more junior employees in the company?

7. Which members of the current team have the skill and will to continue to develop as the organisation grows? Are there roles that exist today that need to enlarge and grow? Are there roles that do not currently exist in the organisation that you need to hire for?

Having asked yourself and the leadership team these questions and answered them honestly, what is your workout plan to help you get from your current state to your future state of organisational muscle? Below are some workouts to help you achieve those plans. You do not need to use every workout. What is important is to focus on the workout that will help you develop the specific organisational muscle that your business requires now and in the future. This will be different for different organisations. The *balance* of organisational muscle to develop is important. Focus too much on speed muscle and you neglect the strength muscle, and vice versa – it's important to focus on both.

Workout Plan

The first challenge with any workout plan is to start immediately! If you identify a capability gap in your leadership team, start hiring for that person today. It takes three to six months to find the right person (at a minimum), and three months to truly on-board the person. It will be at least nine months before you have that extra organisational muscle on board and fully performing at a level that has an impact on the organisation. It is never, ever too early to start hiring for a role – particularly on a leadership team!

1. *Skill/Will Muscle Workout*
    When you are hiring, look for both *skill* and *will muscles* in new employees. Do they have the skill to do the job today and also the willingness to learn new things along the way? Which is more important in an organisation? Both are important, but unless the role is very technical or specialist, if someone has the right attitude, the right approach and a willingness to learn, you can usually teach them most things. If someone has the skill but not the willingness to use that skill or develop further skills, this can be difficult. Learn to develop the organisational muscle to hire the right people with the right mindset!
    At the same time, can you keep building the *passion and enthusiasm muscles?* These are more outward-centred than inward-looking, and infectious. This muscle can be quick and easy to work on, and a good one to start with, because it can easily lead to more muscle growth.
2. *Devolving and Sharing Muscle Workout*
    When you have an able leadership team in place, practice *devolving* and *sharing* muscles to people in the organisation. This is the first step. Develop confidence in your perception of the abilities of others by observation.

3. *'Letting Go' Muscle Workout*

    If your new employees need constant supervision and you
    just can't let go – what's wrong here? Is it your problem or
    theirs? Did you under-hire too much? Have you not delegated
    enough? Are you still obsessive? Are they really not compe-
    tent, or not given a chance? How do you know? Experiment
    … all part of the *letting go muscle*! Is it the end of the world if
    people working autonomously and less controlled by the lead-
    ership team make a few mistakes? How will they learn oth-
    erwise? Building the 'letting people make mistakes' muscle
    without freaking out – it's all part of letting go.

4. *'Feel Like an Owner' Muscle Workout*

    Find someone who is good and then make them feel good
    about joining your organisation. Make them feel like owners
    in the organisation – give them shares, empower them, trust
    them to do the job! Building up this 'feel like an owner' muscle
    is a vital part of you being able to devolve tasks/responsibili-
    ties into the organisation. This is a two-way street – ensure that
    you hire people who want to be empowered and then ensure
    that you empower them.

5. *Trust Muscle Workout*

    Maybe you are still spending a huge amount of time training
    and coaching – you under-hired for the job – and should have
    had more courage, more trust, made a bigger investment in
    a much more capable and experienced person. *Courage and
    trust* are among the most difficult muscles to develop.

6. *Balance Muscle Workout*

    Being less hands-on and stepping back doesn't mean you are
    not committed; it just means you can be *balanced,* which is
    healthy. Stop yourself from jumping in with an opinion and a
    judgement on everything. Deliberately try to keep quiet and
    listen – more often. Lean in to the collective capability of the
    organisation. You have hired talented people – now listen
    to them!

7. *'Being a Coach' Muscle Workout*

    Part of being a leader is also being a coach. Help employees
    set their own development plans so they can grow and
    develop their own individual skill set and muscles. Don't over-
    index on this muscle by spending too much time training and

coaching. Part of being a coach is letting people work things out for themselves. Set employees a task, given them some direction and let them work it out for themselves. You gain time by not micromanaging; they feel empowered to grow and develop. If they make a mistake, trust them to check with you and work on what went well, what did not go so well and how to improve.

Learn to take breaks from work. Go on more holidays, switch off from work. A good workout is followed by a time of rest and *recharging the batteries.* Part of any workout is ensuring that you have time to recover and get ready for the next workout!

2

Workout 2: Anticipating Future Problems – from Solving One at a Time to Coping with Many – from the Here and Now to the Future

- Moving the team's entrepreneurial leadership perspective from the day-to-day to the longer-term – the muscle of anticipating and visualising the future
- From being reactive to proactive, moving from problem-solver to problem-anticipator
- Evolving from real-time single problem-solving to adopting a multiple-perspective problem-solving approach

Part 1: Discussion of the Organisational Muscle to Be Developed

In developing a *future-looking perspective*, we can start by taking a look at the energy model (Krogerus and Tschappeler, 2008), which analyses the balance between tendencies of being memory-, dream- or reality-driven. The team's time-perspective muscle can be any of these – but we suggest that the entrepreneurial leadership muscle, at its most powerful and efficient, is able to exert itself for realistic dreaming, so it can default-juggle between now and the future, informed by the past.

The irony here is that very often, entrepreneurial teams (especially whilst in start-up mode) tend to establish themselves according to the future vision of their product or service and what it will do in the market – in the future. They establish their entrepreneurial venture in a forward-looking, future-envisaged mindset. This is a muscle that most entrepreneurial teams have already developed as they set forth on their adventure. Again, this reminds us of one of our favourite quotes: as Mike Tyson said, 'Everyone has a plan until they get a punch in the face.'

This punch-in-the-face for most entrepreneurial leadership teams on their scale-up journey comes in the form of the day-to-day grind – that is an inevitable part of building and scaling a successful organisation. It's just a fact of entrepreneurial start-up life.

As the organisation moves on, during the journey from start-up to scale-up, the focus tends to switch to the here and now. There is a certain excitement about today, so much so that sometimes we can forget about tomorrow – and forget about the longer-term plan. Nobody now has the time or mental resources to think about tomorrow. The start-up dreams start fading away …

So, many start-up entrepreneurs and their teammates can be so concentrated on the present and the day-to-day excitement of coping with whatever is being thrown at them that they can't think of more than a few days or weeks ahead. The Blue Ocean or Blue Sky stuff has become rather distant. Cash flow, buying essential daily supplies and negotiating with the bank to have enough cash to pay the bills – all these tend to stop the possibility of future-planning in its tracks. But – and this is not necessarily realised at the time – being trapped in the here and now can make being scaled up seem like an increasingly impossible dream.

Thus, the first challenge in this workout emerges as this muscle is identified. How do we, as an entrepreneurial team, live and survive and thrive today and simultaneously dream, plan and organise for tomorrow? The inevitable dichotomy of balance emerges. How to lead, manage and operate in two different time frames at the same time? How do we create the delicate balancing act of focusing on what will move the needle today and also what will move the needle tomorrow? It's not easy, but that muscle is there and just needs to be exercised and developed.

This 'realistic-dreaming' muscle needs to be built up and kept going and work for a purpose – and here we are talking about developing the muscle to widen the ability to multi-problem-solve. It's not just about increasing the speed and endurance of running on the treadmill but doing upper-body exercises at the same time and building coordination and motor-skills – physically and mentally. So, this workout starts with building the muscle to anticipate the future – from the here and now to strategizing long-term.

This leads us onto the second challenge in this particular muscle group: moving from celebrating the 'problem-solver' moment to empowering the 'problem-anticipator' ability. It's there – it just needs to be exercised. From taking on one problem to several – it's a stretch, but it's possible.

Meanwhile, typical organisations founded today (especially in such a time of rapid change) are often addressing a defined business need or identified business problem to be solved which has recently emerged. Start-up organisations thrive on and celebrate organisational 'heroes' who can solve problems and then move on to solving the next challenge. This tends to be reactive rather than proactive. This takes us to the third challenge in this workout – the third of the three muscles to be worked on.

This reactive-and-responsive capability is an important organisational muscle to have at the early stage of the start-up journey. It can be particularly prevalent in technology-focused organisations, where a 'test and learn' mantra is common. Releasing products with potentially known or unknown issues is a trade-off for getting the product or service to market as quickly as possible. The strategy is to deliberately release a version of the product or service into the market that is not fully vetted but, through the process, get real-time feedback from customers and users, to change, evolve and enhance the product or service on a continual basis.

However, as the organisation grows and scales, this muscle can be overused and overstretched. Not all employees thrive on solving problems requiring reaction, and meanwhile customers who were forgiving of known problems with service at the start (they were the early adopters and were warned as such) can now be less forgiving of issues, bugs or challenges with a product or service. A significant amount of organisational energy and resources can be used up addressing reactive problems. This is not the way to go in the future, and not the way to develop a sustainable scaled-up business. Reactivity must be transformed into proactivity – sooner rather than later.

An inflection point towards becoming something bigger and better comes when organisations need to move to anticipating and solving future potential organisational problems upfront rather than reactively and retroactively addressing the challenges. Again, this is not a sudden shift in organisational momentum – it is an organisational muscle that needs to be developed all along the journey. Often, this is an organisational capability that does not necessarily exist within the current framework of the organisation and is most likely to be needed to be acquired and augmented from external sources. If it's not there, it needs to be brought in.

Both of these issues – looking to the future and proactivity – cause us to identify another complementary muscle that needs to be developed. In the problem- solving, live-for-today mindset, the organisation often thrives on individuals solving one problem at a time. As discussed above, the heroic problem-solving muscle is celebrated and the problem-anticipator muscle is often underutilised and under-celebrated (and therefore underdeveloped and under-exercised).

This often leads to problems being identified individually, rather than systemically. Adopting a 'systems thinking' approach to this issue not only identifies current problems but also anticipates future problems. This complementary muscle thus nicely dovetails with the future-thinking, proactive muscle in a very systematic way, to help move the organisation further along on its journey to scale-up.

As we have seen, an inevitable challenge of future-thinking is the need to move from solving one problem at a time to creating/addressing/solving *multiple problems* (the second muscle element). The future will never be linear. Thus, rather than just focusing on solving problems in the here and now, with the development of the muscle to strategize for the future, the related muscle of multi-problem-solving needs to be toned and exercised too. They must all be worked on and exercised in the same workout.

With that power to focus on the future and multi-problem-solve, the workout continues to build the strength to let go of reactivity to problems – from simply responding to creating. This muscle group includes *building proactivity*, taking initiative, being open to new ideas, creating and living with a vision for the future – which may involve challenging the status quo. It's one of the early muscle sets to develop on the journey to being a top-performing entrepreneurial leadership team (and is our essential third muscle element).

However, one of the challenges here is to ensure that we still use the problem-solving, think-for-today, reactive muscle. That must not be neglected as we scale and grow. In any organisation, and particularly in an organisation growing and scaling in this way, this will still be a vital organisational muscle to have fully developed and ready to be used when needed and kept in good shape.

The beauty of this workout regime is that these are very complementary muscles, and the organisational capability both to develop this type of muscle internally and to augment current capability with external capability will be an important balance to strike. The organisation must act as a system and as a unit think along two different time frames at the same time – like a sprinter and a long-distance runner:

– Sprints: Running short distances, very fast in as little time as possible, thinking just about the finish line. Technique and processes can be sacrificed just to get to the finish line.
– Marathons: Running long distances, at a slower but still very fast pace, allowing time to reflect and think while getting to the finish line, staying in the race and making the distance. The right systems processes and techniques are important to stay in the race and make the distance.

This muscle workout then leads logically to muscle Workout 3 – looking inside the organisation and building its capability rather than just looking at customers, Workout 4 – taking on different organisational roles and evolving, Workout 5 – coping with a different and more challenging kind of risk,

Workout 6 – leading the inevitable culture change, and Workout 7 – building a growth mindset for the years to come.

Without Workouts 1 and 2 – letting go of personal autonomy, developing teamwork, and anticipating and embracing future challenges – the succeeding workouts lack a foundation of prior preparation, fitness and power.

Thus, we need Workout 2 – future-looking, multi-problem-managing and building up from reactivity to proactivity. Go for it!

We have identified the organisational muscle that we need to work out at this point. Let's now hear from some of the entrepreneurial leaders we have spoken to in our research for this book – and how they talk about the challenges of building this organisational muscle.

Part 2: Experiences of Entrepreneurial Leaders – Anticipating the Future, Mono-problem-Solver to Multi-problem-Solver, and from eing Reactive to Proactive

The Future-Looking Perspective

The second muscle workout in our series of seven is geared towards the entrepreneurial leadership team evolving from focusing purely on what is happening in the next 24 hours to starting to build a vision for the future. The aim in developing this muscle is to ensure that you can build strength in the immediate short term as well as the longer term. As discussed earlier, the irony here is that often this is a muscle that is in place as the venture gets underway but becomes underutilised and atrophies as the organisation focuses more on the issues right in front of them, here and now. It's hard to think about next year when all your organisational energy and resource is focused on getting through this week! The balance here is to 'reactivate' this muscle when it's needed and keep developing it. In practice, this often means that this muscle is currently present in the organisation and bringing on board other capabilities to manage the day-to-day is often a way to allow the organisation to focus on this complementary muscle; future- and here-and-now thinking – they go together. The entrepreneurs we interviewed realised the importance of this, but many struggled at the same time – to simultaneously let go of the day-to-day and revive their focus on thinking longer-term, which they had been doing all along ...

> Encouraging everyone to *think future* – it's about being honest and it's about just getting everyone to understand the vision, to share the problem, what we're trying to do, helping them to think it through and see it. And I tend to find most of the people were just really motivated and loyal just by me being passionate about the vision and explaining about the challenges that we had.
>
> I think you must keep stating the *vision* for the company, making sure you're going in the right direction, making sure you're outperforming the market.
>
> It's about your ability to inspire with a *vision* ... that we're trying to get to from A to B, come follow me on that. We need to keep working on that future perspective.
>
> *Vision* made real – my own personal experience is that it's so easy to get excited about the idea of setting up a company and running a company, but the actual reality of doing it is miles different and it involves a huge range of skills and things that you're not aware of at the start, unless, I guess, you're a genius or somebody actual told you all about it.
>
> We need to understand *future realities* and keep moving with the times.
>
> With the need for *future success*, it's really about making sure you deliver the bacon, deliver the wealth creation ... whether it's earnings or other deliverables, you measure milestones. Need to keep thinking of the next moves.
>
> We now look at the strategy and *future opportunities*, as we have put in place someone taking care of putting out fires happening now.
>
> We take care of both today and tomorrow together; I care mainly for the strategy for the future; I delegate the day-to-day to someone else.
>
> It happens more often; we talk about our *future* vision, we have young professionals so it's easier to communicate ideas and the team makes it happen fast.
>
> Our *vision* is not entirely the same now as it was – once we grew it was hard to pass the same vision to everyone – we were growing

so fast – it was not so easy to explain the vision and keep pushing it with a larger organisation – and I know I need to do more work on this thinking about the future.

In terms of the *future vision*: I go for it, I have lots of ideas and I always want to test them; normally I talk it over with my partners and we fine-tune it. There have been successes and failures, but I enjoy bringing them to life.

Being Future-Oriented – the Challenge

For most entrepreneurial leaders, this is a muscle they often recognise as needing to be reactivated or developed. Either because they don't yet have the right day-to-day organisational capability present in the company yet or, perhaps deep down, they secretly thrive on the hustle-and-bustle of the day-to-day, the future-orientated perspective can be very challenging for them – to give it the right amount of focus it needs.

It's not easy to be future-oriented ... I would say that at this stage I am still handling mostly our everyday issues and don't have much time to think about the future. But I do realize that I will need to before long.

Both *current and future* challenges are important. I would say I try to anticipate what will happen next as much as I can, but inevitably I get involved in day-to-day issues when needed, which is still often.

I thrive during difficult times. To me flexibility is the name of the game. I did not worry much about the future, as long as we had plenty of business ... but this did mean that I was mostly in the *here and now*.

The team is not developed enough yet; they need the owner to be there for the work to get done up to my standard, so *I can't yet think ahead.*

I try to look mainly at the future, but I can't ignore day-to-day issues. I have to make it work *taking care of both.* It's a balancing act.

It's *more difficult to plan ahead*, if I want something to happen it takes longer. I also attribute it to the company being still young; we are still testing at this stage, and just like any other new company, we are still stuck in the here and now.

I look at both now and what we need to do in the future; they are *both important.*

It doesn't happen often. We mostly get on with what we are doing now, but we still might have a new idea for the future, and in the end we adapt to the *vision*, even if it's in the background and we don't think about it every day.

Our vision is gradually working out, but we had to overcome a lot of obstacles – we are now more successful in converting people to the vision – both customers and staff members – but we had to give up on some of the old retainers – the team has to be with us. We can't have people undermining us as we go along.

Moving from Mono-problem-Solving to Multi-problem- or Systemic Problem-Solving

Many entrepreneurial leadership teams set up their businesses on a mono-problem or one specific pain point which they have clearly identified. Already in the organisation's DNA can be the idea of being the 'problem-solver' – and this can become part of a celebrated cultural norm. Often, the profile of the new employees – those whom the entrepreneurial leadership team brings on board – is focused on helping them to solve these current problems. Thus, structurally the founders of the start-up hire a problem-solver into a problem-solving context and culture, and then continuously celebrate and laud the problem-solver as the hero. No wonder that problem-solving becomes an inherent part of 'what success looks like around here'. However, as the organisation grows and scales, it is not sufficient to just solve problem after problem. This can turn into a game of whack-a-mole. The organisation needs to shift to solve multiple problems at the same time. This can be quite an organisational shift for the culture to undergo, and then it's quite a shift to move to multiple problems – especially when it's more than the start-up team can handle.

> Starting with a *one-problem* focus, the biggest thing was detecting a pain point that nobody was willing to solve. Either the pain point was too small for a large company to bother to try to solve, or the pain point was so big that nobody wanted to attempt it. It took too much intestinal fortitude to try to solve the problem. But somebody should be able to do it. Realising that there's no somebody, and then that I should be able to do it, was the motivation.

> Most of being an entrepreneur is five or six days of dead air followed by one day of joy. What *motivates* good entrepreneurs is if you see some happiness with customers ... when you see

your customer really progress in their business when you are helping them, you are enabling another business to do something interesting.

I wanted to do more for the customer and I just saw the opportunity of what needed to be done. So it is much more about solving a *problem* that either I came across or I experienced, and I just wanted to solve that particular problem.

But there's a need to move on from there, from handling *one problem too many* ...

Problem-solving is what I do, it has decreased but I have been battling against the old ways of my family business and I have now won considerable ground with them. Today I believe we have achieved success in the local market, but I am still aiming to take our products to the international market.

If you want to be a big company, solve *big problems*. If you want to be a small company, solve small problems.

At the beginning my vision was of a much bigger scale, but now I realise that the quality of my services is what differentiates me. It's a personal choice to keep the company small rather than getting it bigger. So I'm still mostly working on *one problem at a time.*

Our vision was to create a small but value-adding unique business and then keep it going ... until we didn't want to do it anymore ... we liked the *problem-solving* work for new clients best, but we are happy to work with those who just want to keep us on retainer – so we like the new visionary work but we need the day-to-day stuff.

My work initially consisted of helping *bailing out my clients with problems* and this changed a bit over time, as the clients moved into maintaining their strategies rather than starting them from scratch, then it was less problematic. But there were always new customers and a need to keep marketing. And no customers were interested unless they had to be.

Problem-solving is a big part; we have a huge focus on solving our *customer's issues.* I consider myself the main bridge in connecting customer's needs to my workers. In recent years I have designated a person to help me with the recurring problems, but I am still mostly responsible of solving new everyday problems. My phone registered that last week I spent 48 hours on the phone talking to my clients and my workers. I am certainly moving in the direction of multi-problem-solving.

Around six months ago, I *deliberately zoned out of direct customer problem-solving* and the local partner took over this, while I focus on running our head office operations with a much more strategic role, looking at shared objectives, creating teams, projects and new revenue streams, more concerned with the financial part of the business.

Moving from the Reactive to the Proactive

Another important and complementary muscle workout involves anticipating and predicting problems to be solved, rather than just working on problems as they turn up – this represents another transitional moment on the path from start-up to scaled-up. Putting out fires all day is not what makes a sustainable business. The organisation needs to shift from solving the problem to anticipating the problem in the first place. It is not always an easy transformation:

Being *proactive*, creative and *making opportunities* – I think the notion of creating value and creating something out of nothing is quite interesting. To have a blank sheet of paper and then a year down the line you're employing 10 people, you have a certain amount of revenue coming in, and that has started from nothing, from absolute zero. So that concept of a magical appearance out of thin air I think is fascinating.

We are all millennials and we all ended up in big companies … where we quickly realised this is not for us. And a lot of my friends and now business partners felt the same way. They wanted an alternative opportunity. We wanted to be doing our own thing. We needed to keep being *proactive*.

We are trying to anticipate *future problems* by monitoring where it's going – I get all the information where we're heading, how much money we have, who's happy and who's not happy, what clients we have. It's not easy, but once you have all the information, it's much easier to make a decision.

Every idea that is submitted is taken into account and discussed by the management team. There's a lot of room for our own initiative in the business, and we are all thinking about what happens next. We want to *manage that process*, not let it just sort of happen.

I consider myself an innovator. I really like bringing ideas to life and this is actually part of the service I offer my clients – I want to help them with solutions that can make their business grow. So I'm always looking to the *next exciting new thing*.

I saw an opportunity when we started. I believed in what we could accomplish with this project – that is why I have passionately invested my time and money in it. I could see the *potential* good we could do with it.

I am just looking at our future. We do not pursue size or power; we aspire to be a good company that will last for 102 years. We aim to build the future infrastructure of commerce in a *proactive* and dynamic way.

Strategy is very much what I do. It's a race to beat the other firms and serve the clients faster than anyone else. I have developed some really good processes. It was a big investment. But this means I can do the work faster and more efficiently than my competitors. This is what I set out to do and I'm *still working on improving* it.

Our original vision is working out, but we are still struggling to realize the implications of it becoming a reality. At least we are trying to be *proactive and slowly getting there.*

I think my vision worked out well. I have a nice business, it could be more – but I'm still *working on it.* I'm quite *restless* about it.

One of the reasons I managed to be successful at the beginning was because I made a point of *going through with my ideas;* they did not always run smoothly, but it is worse to be doing nothing new. I always tried to be proactive.

I approach each future plan with my methodology. I *set my idea in motion,* and depending on the initial response or feedback I change it accordingly.

Having heard the voices of the entrepreneurial leaders as they looked to understand how they developed or reactivated the muscle around moving from day to day to thinking about tomorrow, moving from reactive to proactive mode and also moving from mono-problem-solving to multi-problem-solving, let's now move to focus on the specific questions to address the current state of this organisational muscle and then some specific workouts to develop that muscle.

Part 3: Workout Practice – Moving from the Current State to the Future State

- Understand the current and necessary future state of this organisational muscle.
- Through this, identify the organisational muscle to be developed.

- Then put in place a workout plan to develop the muscle – with milestones, targets and regular check-ins on whether the muscle is being developed – and the result is seven key workouts within Workout 2 to develop this particular organisational muscle.
- Practising simple exercises regularly will build strength here – in Workout 2 it's all about transforming three different but related parts of the entrepreneurial leadership team's body.
- The team as a whole needs to work on this muscle at the same time for it to be effective – not just the individuals.
- These muscle groups are interconnected in the body and need to work in harmony with each other.

The purpose of the seven key questions below is to get the organisational leadership team to think about the following:
How much focus do we put on day-to-day versus future planning?

How much are we reactive as an organisation rather than pro-active – how much we do problem-solve rather than anticipate the problem?

How much do we focus on the mono-problem (the problem in front of us) rather than thinking about problems as a system or in a multi-problematic way?

Here are the seven key questions to assess the current organisational muscle for Workout 2:

1. What types of conversations are the leadership team in the organisation having? Analyse the conversations – and the team's thought process and decision-making styles. Use an outside observer or make a recording and then dissect it. What does it mean?

   - What percentage of the discussion is about now?
   - What percentage of the discussion is about the past?
   - What percentage of the discussion is about the future?

   Based on where you are as an organisation, what percentage of time should be devoted at leadership meetings to the here and now, and what percentage of time should be devoted to future planning/strategy?

2. Future vision: As an organisation, do you have a clear vision about the future? Is there clear alignment of this vision by all members of the leadership team? Has the vision been clearly communicated to all employees, and is it clearly understood by all people in the organisation?

    As you hire additional employees into the organisation, do you clearly communicate this vision to them? If you ask five employees about what the vision of the organisation is – what the direction of the organisation is – what answer do you get?

3. As you encounter problems/issues/challenges in your organisation, how do you solve them? Think hard: How do you really solve them? Do you tend to solve the problem right in front of you and move on to the next problem? Do you solve in a mono-problem way – one problem at a time? Or do you think of future implications?

4. *Who* solves the problems in the organisation? Is problem-solving devolved throughout the organisation, or are problems solved by the same people? Are these people subject-matter experts in the organisation, or are they just the more senior people in the organisation? Who decides?

    Is problem-solving spread equally among the team, or is it just a small cohort of people who can solve the problem? Or is it that others could but are not invited to do so?

5. Are problems in the organisation solved in a reactive or pro-active way – that is, does the organisation wait for problems/issues/challenges to emerge, or do they actively look for problems? Does the organisation stress-test how it works, how it gets things done? What if you had to shift the product faster, or produce more units? As you scale, do you know at what point your processes and ways of doing things will break down? Is it at 1,000, 10,000 or 100,000 units?

6. Are you truly anticipating the problems you will need to solve in the future? Do you have a way of identifying future problems? If not, why not? And what are you going to do now? If you do, do you look to find a solution now, or are you happy that you have just found a future problem – that at least you have thought about it?

7. Do you celebrate the problem-solving 'hero' in the organisation – the person who worked all night to solve a particular

bug or particular product issue? Do you 'institutionalise' the hero as to 'how we do things around here'? How do you celebrate the person who anticipates the issues and addresses them before they become a problem? Or do you not even think about them? Are you hooked on the adrenaline of continuously putting out fires rather than looking to see how you can put the right ways of doing things in place so that you don't have to constantly put out fires?

By asking these probing questions of the organisation, you can then help the leadership team to focus on the specific organisational muscles that they need to work out. Below are the suggested workouts to develop and activate each of the muscles identified in this particular workout.

Workout Plan

1. *Leadership Team Future Discussion Muscle Workout*
   Analyse the conversations the leadership team is having – and their thought process and decision-making styles. Use an outside observer, or make a recording and then dissect it. Based on your observations as a leadership team, make a conscious choice about what percentage of time should be devoted to discussing future discussions about the organisation. This can be future planning, future strategy or future products. Decide how you want to do this – you might devote a percentage of your time at each of your regular weekly or monthly conversations to doing this, or you might decide that you need to dedicate a half- or a full day once a quarter. There is no right or wrong answer with this muscle – just a conscious decision on which muscle you wish to develop or trade-off.

2. *Organisational Vision Muscle Workout*
   This is about understanding the vision of the organisation – how often as a leadership team do you discuss the vision/ direction of the organisation? Is this muscle developed enough? Do you speak about this vision regularly at your all-hands/all-employee meetings? Conduct a survey in the organisation – either formally or informally – and ask people how

well they understand the vision. Ask them to write down the vision. Take a close look at the results. If you have a clearly understood vision by all employees, then keep doing what you are doing to continue to develop this muscle. If you don't, put in place a plan to regularly communicate the vision and have employee Q&A sessions on the vision of the organisation. Decide who has ownership and accountability for this plan. As you grow and hire more employees into your organisation, this muscle needs to be continually developed and worked on.

3.   *Aligned Organisation Muscle Workout*
Go on team awaydays. Get out of the office to a completely new environment. It could be on a ship at sea, up a mountain, in a retreat, in a medieval castle – but it must be equally new for everyone, with no associations with the past or present. Devote 100 per cent of that day to thinking about the future. Hire an experienced external facilitator to guide the decision. Come away from the day with a clear set of actions that will help you achieve your organisation's vision. Refresh and re-focus the organisational vision on a regular basis!

4.   *Vocabulary to Make It Work*
Then, when you talk about the future-thinking you did that day, you'll have a name for it – the ship, the mountain, the monastery or the castle. Reliving the experience will keep you all focused on reliving the dream and making it happen, even when bogged down with the problems of today. Do this on a regular basis – at least once a year!

5.   *Proactive Problem-Solving Muscle Workout*
Identify who in the organisation is solving the problems. Get data-driven on this. Put in place a log of all problems solved. This will give the team an insight into who is solving them and what types of problems are being solved. Analyse this data for patterns that can help you develop the organisational problem-solving muscle. As you roll out a new product or service, put in place a 'pre-mortem' – identify what you think are some of the issues that will arise. Put in place a detailed plan to address these issues. Get proactive and get ahead of problems, challenges and issues. Afterwards, have a 'post-mortem' – what was similar between the pre- and the post-mortem? What

was different? What did the organisation learn about proactive problem-solving that you can bring to the next iteration of the product or service?

6. *Reactive Problem-Solving Muscle Workout*
    Conversely, identify who in the organisation is accountable for causing the problem. Note, this is not a witch-hunt! This is to develop the muscle on *why* problems are needing to be solved – is it a lack of time, a lack of resources or a lack of expertise or capability? By systematically doing this, you will identify which specific muscle you need to develop. If it is time or resources, what is the plan to create more time or add more resources? If it is expertise, put in place a specific plan to develop this expertise, either internally or through augmenting from external sources. Either grow the muscle or buy the muscle, but either way, develop the muscle!

7. *Balancing the 'Hero' Muscle Workout*
    Do you over-index on 'celebrate the hero problem-solving muscle'? What is the plan to develop the 'anticipate the problem before it becomes a problem' muscle? Do you need to change the profile of the people you are hiring into the organisation? Write down how many 'problem-solver' heroes you have in the organisation, and then write down the number of 'anticipate the problem' solvers you have. Do they balance? Do they get equal visibility and lauding across the company? What you celebrate as an organisation becomes the accepted behaviour for others to emulate. Move from problem-solving to problem-anticipating as an organisational behaviour. If not, you need to put in place a plan to hire more of the 'anticipate the problem' solvers … right away!

So now the team – with finely honed future-oriented, multi-problem-focused and proactivity muscles – can move your business from a simple start-up (not quite sure where it's going) to a sustainable, fast-growing, scaled-up business with future clarity and ambidexterity. It's time to move on to Workout 3!

3

Workout 3: Changing Your Focus – from Being Customer-Driven to Problem-Solving 360° – from Looking Outside to Looking Inside

- Moving from an external focus – in terms of looking mostly at customers and opportunities – to also looking at how to manage the business internally
- Widening the focus of the business, from the initial idea, which may have centred round just a small group of customers and products or services, to something much more – and developing resources to take on a bigger mandate
- Changing the business direction to move with new opportunities, to take on bigger problems in a more holistic way – and to build teams to cope with these challenges
- Adapting to the changing drivers of the business – from serving a group of customers to addressing the whole sector – and in the process evolving the business to address changing needs – to manage the organizational capability to respond

Part 1: Discussion of the Organisational Muscle to Be Developed

Most companies today profess to obsess about the customer. This customer obsession and focus is evident in hugely successful organisations like Amazon ('still day one'), and most companies place a lot of emphasis on putting customers at the heart of decision-making around their product or service. Having a strong customer focus mentality is key to an organisation gaining the initial market momentum. Often (and specifically in the entrepreneurial businesses of the leaders we have spoken to in our research) a huge driver of setting up a company or a venture was that the founding team had found a gap in the market that was not at the time being served by other organisations, or they had discovered a particular pain point for customers which they thought they could solve. Thus, customer obsession, and a focus on the customer, is often a driver for why organisations are established in the first place. This is particularly relevant for organisations which are in the technology space.

This is often taken a step further by many organisations, as they actively involve and collaborate with their customers in the development process of the product or service they are planning to bring to market. It is quite common (particularly in technology-focused organisations) to bring a not-quite-finished version of the product to market (a 'beta' product, or a 'pilot' product or service). The deliberate choice and trade-off is to bring a 'not fully polished' version to market and see how well it lands, and to actively ask customers and clients to use the product and then give immediate feedback on the product or service – and how it can be improved. It's testing and trying out in real time.

This is often linked to a problem-solving scenario, as early adopters of a product or service are actively encouraged to give feedback on the product or service. This feedback loop with the customer allows the organisation to refine/review their product offering to the user, building loyalty and commitment in the process. By actively involving the end consumer, these companies and teams have a strong customer focus to build the product that the customers really desire and actively want. The customer also feels like they have 'skin in the game'. This strategy can be immensely powerful when it comes to solving particular pain points for customers, as the organisation instantly gets feedback on what features of the product or service they can tweak, add, modify or delete, to finally bring a more refined version of the product to market. This is an especially important organisational muscle for companies to develop, and most customers (at least initially) spend time and energy on this, so early in the company's journey, this can be a muscle that can become very well developed.

However, there is an important flip side to this equation. In order to deliver on the customer feedback, the organisation will also need to ensure that they have paid sufficient attention to their own internal capability muscle. This internal capability needs to be developed in order to deliver on the customers' needs, desires and feedback – but this might occur at the expense of resources that could be or used to be directed at the external customer muscle. This balancing act is at the heart of Workout 3.

Workout 3 looks at an important inflection point as an organisation moves from start-up to scale-up mode. Organisational and customer growth is a wonderful thing. However, a point occurs when the organisation scales up and the customer feedback and input grow, and the business has to address and solve the wishes and desires of an increasing number of customers, far more than they had to before.

Additionally, what is often seen is that the external customer-interface muscle is rather well developed in the organisation, but the internal organisational muscle or capability to *deliver* on the customers' needs, for the sustainable long term, is rather less evident. This is akin to a swimmer focusing more on one arm for their swimming stroke and less on the other arm. They can still effectively swim from one end of the pool to the other, but not as efficiently or effectively as if they focused on both arms at the same time. Or they could manage one length of the pool quite quickly, but two or more lengths would be a rather different matter. Having found the customers and promised them a product or service, the organisation now needs to deliver on that promise. It can easily be a case of overpromised and under-delivered. An equilibrium needs to be reached in terms of organisational muscle to deliver on the promise or else risk the ire of the customer!

The company could face two main issues at this point. It might have constrained resources and it needs to make a trade-off by switching some resources from the external customer-growth aspect of the organisation to the internal customer-delivery capability. Or it might be in another position, where it has the capability to fund additional resources in order to further develop this internal-focused muscle but may not know how to go about it, and how to make the choices. Either way, the organisation needs to begin the process of further building the right internal systematic organisational capability (systems, processes and procedures) to deliver the product or service to the customer. This is an important realignment that needs to occur before true scale-up can be on the cards. Again, the organisational muscle used to focus on the customer externally cannot easily adapt to the need to balance this with growing organisational capability to deliver for the customer. This is often seen in the tensions and trade-offs between the organisational sales team (give the customer what they want, to drive revenue) and the internal product or service team who are tasked with building, developing or refining the product (at what cost do we deliver the product?). The sales muscle versus the product/service delivery muscle has raised its head. How to manage both?

Another issue can arise at this stage – in the mad dash to gain market traction and customer growth: the organisation might not yet have developed the muscle to understand the needs of the customer. More specifically, do we have a 360° view of the customer to gain insight into the overall customer picture? Maybe not. Often, the organisation has a clear view on the dollar revenue that a specific customer or set of customers could bring in. However, they might be much less clear on what might be the acquisition costs and the ongoing costs associated with that customer. How much discount did it cost to acquire that customer? How much internal resources are we spending on customising the product or service for that particular customer? How often does the customer have issues/challenges with the product or service? How often do they call the customer support helpline? All of this is a cost to the business, so having a clear view of this is important in measuring costs.

For many organisations, as they try to scale up, this is often not a key area of focus – this is often not a muscle that they feel (or even know) that they need to develop. Developing this 360° view of the customer is an important organisational muscle to build – without it, scale-up cannot work effectively. The sales muscle can overwhelm the product-delivery muscle – to the longer-term detriment of the organisation.

For many organisations, as they grow and scale, this inflection point can often bring tensions to both the founding leadership team and the organisation. It can be an important moment to pause and reflect to understand whether they have the right capability, the right balance, on both the leadership team and across the organisation in order to navigate through the various trade-off decisions that will need to be made. Like all trade-off decisions on the journey from start-up to scale-up in the organisation, there is no specific right or wrong answer. It's what works.

Part 2: Experiences of Entrepreneurial Leaders – External and Internal Focus

In this section, as always, we will look to the voices and experiences of the entrepreneurial leaders that we have spoken to as research for this book. Let's hear their views on how they have managed through the external and internal focus tension, how to incorporate the external landscape into the internal organisation of the company, how to delegate and how to transition the organisation between the two. These are, of course, challenges for the organisation, as the experiences of our entrepreneurial leaders will testify to. Let us understand those challenges in their own words.

The Tendency to Keep Focused Externally – It's Hard to Let Go

> I keep looking at the *external market* mainly; I am always looking for potential opportunities all the time.
> I am always looking at the outside; the *inside takes time and it will eventually be sorted out.* But you need to worry about the

outside – what can you offer your customer, what other opportunities can I take advantage of?

I have to look at both, but my main focus at the time *is the outside*. I really enjoy talking to potential customers, and offering our services.

I had always the vision to look for the opportunities nobody else was exploiting, which is how I created my business and also the reason we became successful. Now that we are bigger I let *somebody else take care of internal matters*. I do get involved, but my main focus is looking to our future and possibilities – still on the outside.

I prefer *focusing on the customers* and the outside. I know how important it is but I don't like dealing with the internal works of the business; I always look to designate someone to help me with this or seek out partners with experience in this.

For me it is important to look at both parts: On the *inside you need formats and processes*; standardization is important so that you don't need to repeat every project from zero every time and so that your employees can work within the same processes. As for the external part, it is important to grow it and look for new clients so you don't get stuck without growing.

They are both important, inside and outside, but the biggest concern is tactical operation and keeping your business growing. You *look at the internal structure* because you have to but that is not your priority; it is always about how you can grow your business. You do not grow because of your structure.

I am mainly looking at external opportunities to continue developing our product; at the beginning I used to be more involved in the growing and scaling-up of the company, but this job has been taken over by other members of the founding team. I can now work on doing more of what I like – and *others do the internal* management stuff.

Making the Transition – Launching the Process

At the beginning you have more time and focus on the biggest chances to grow the business. To be honest, at the beginning what you are focused on is making enough money to pay yourself and get the jobs done. Now that we have grown, there's people who are in charge of that and *we can focus the on the internal structure and strategy*, building the company itself. The shift has been recent. Three to four years ago we still were externally focused and it's just recently that we are focusing on internal issues. I like working on the operational side of the business, but I believe it will be better for me to focus on the strategy now.

I started looking at the market. I could see the future potential of my business, then when I had to actually start to figure out the whole operation, the employees, the way we work, how my family managed the business compared to what I wanted to do with it, *all my energy shifted to our internal structure*, but I never lost sight of us growing up; I just had to learn how to manage both expectations.

At the beginning it was all about marketing the services. I did open days, created some successful campaigns, established connections with important business people who could potentially be interested in us, and once we started getting a regular clientele I had to look for more support to get the job done, so I started *developing the business internally*, and I hired some staff and developed a partner network.

At the start I wanted to get back my investment fast, so I heavily marketed our business. We were profitable for a long time, and eventually I was forced to start *managing the business from the inside*, which wasn't my real interest. But the few staff we had liked my hands-off style and laid-back approach. Since it was a small business, it more or less managed itself, although it was always a bit chaotic and policy decisions were made when and where they were needed.

First of all, I definitely just looked at the potential to start my own business. I was working in an international firm branch and I knew I could do it by myself. I just had to get enough clients to keep me going at the start. That was all I could think about. When I thought the time was right, I told my clients I was setting up on my own, offered them a slightly cheaper deal, and they came with me. But then, when I started hiring staff, and looking at infrastructure I could use, I *was much more focused on internal issues*. This is a fast-turnover business; people come and go, and I knew they would, so I had to keep hiring new people. Also some of my people left and took clients with them, just like I did.

Making the Transition – Tracking the Process

Back in 2016 my main focus were my customers. As a tech guy with experience as a freelancer, in the first days of my company I was out connected to the market and getting us clients. Now my focus is different; I'm working on systems to make my business sustainable and scalable. *I keep track of our performance* – I have a tool measuring ROI for everything.

When I started my only focus was surviving and trying to make money. We have stabilized the business now but I am struggling to standardize it, and the *implementation of structures* has been difficult.

I look at both the inside and the outside because I am the owner, but my partner focuses on sales – and he is a natural at that. I can absolutely handle them too but that's the way we split it. The way I contribute is with my technology expertise; I can talk business and offer solutions to our clients being able to explain it. But I would say that my role demands me more to be in charge of *operations within the company.*

Adopting Some Corporate Features

In a corporate environment – and there are generalisations, some of which are true, some of which aren't true – I found that the developed corporate culture can sometimes be a hindrance to the people. So you can sometimes have entrepreneurial leaders in corporates, and unfortunately, they almost always have to make *a choice.* Being inward- or outward-looking.

If you are finding it hard to look inwards and need to *delegate to team members who can build functions* in a business, I think you should ask for forgiveness, not permission, and have to deal with the consequences. So that maybe an entrepreneurial leader can thrive and hopefully, because of what they've done, they can prove that through asking for forgiveness, actually, what they've done has been fantastic, even though more risky. And make the way for *others to focus on developing the business.*

Many entrepreneurial leaders are *stifled in a corporate* because of things that are very natural in corporate environments. If it's one piece of software, for example, you want that to be used ubiquitously. So that needs to have a lot of sign-offs from a lot of people and that's completely normal; you have to get permission. Entrepreneurial leaders hate this stuff, they just want to get going with the customers.

Many entrepreneurial leadership teams are often not very experienced in entrepreneurial environments or they are way more technical, or have different skill sets. They don't want to be in a corporate environment, but they don't know much about being on their own. The scaling won't happen at the same level or rate as it might at a more mature company, so you see leaders get *pushed way out of their comfort zones* and gain experience more quickly. They have to adjust.

I think a lot of the people I've met who are coming in from taking a corporate job find it incredibly hard to be successful as an entrepreneur in business, and I don't think they ever appreciated how *difficult* it was. Especially the balancing of looking inside and outside.

For the most part, I also think that entrepreneurial organisations are more accepting and *forgiving* ... than in large corporates, in terms of what that ramp period of growth might look like or the conditions where you consider it failure; it's more flexible, you must be able to cope with ambiguity. Not all entrepreneurial leaders can cope with this, although they are attracted to the idea.

In the more mature organisations there is a *narrower range of acceptable leadership behaviour,* or the criteria for what makes a leader in the established cultural environment is much clearer, they are much more quick to say that this person's out, or that this person's someone we want to continue working with.

In entrepreneurial organisations, anything goes. The people who have come from corporates who wanted to be entrepreneurs often find this transition much harder than they expected. They might be better at the *internal than the external* tasks.

In a large organisation, if you do anything that's considered *tactical,* you're seen as a weak leader. So you do everything you can to spend all your time doing *strategic* work or doing large-scale work. In a small company, in a very start-up environment, you have to do all the tactical things or you cannot have a conversation about anything strategic because the tactical things are what are going to kill you. So if you're unable to actually do some of those tactical things, you're not going to be successful. So in that way, it's different. It's a balance between two perspectives.

Understanding the Outside and Inside Worlds

Corporate organisations have to make an active effort to *manage the external context* in which they were operating, and consciously doing this can have beneficial consequences for the internal organisation. Start-ups can be the other way around.

Managing the *external environment* enables entrepreneurial leaders to gather intelligence about what was happening in the marketplace – then they have to think about how to serve that market.

We heard a cautionary tale of how not consciously paying
attention to your *external leadership brand* can also have a
potentially negative impact on how the organisation is viewed
in the context of the wider external marketplace. So being
externally focused has its pluses.

We had quite a well-thought-through process about what people
can be *seeing from the outside world.* That included how we come
across as our brand and in our product and how we present
ourselves across any form of communications. That was
culturally embedded in what we did.

It's that vision, and the good entrepreneurial leaders can do
external-facing stuff. Good at PR and price, good at attracting
investment. Today, if you really want to grow quickly, you
need some people to believe that you can do it. They're good
at that kind of networking, good at knowing the right
people, and bringing them on board as a member raising
money really helps. Then you can build an organization
around it.

An important part of being an owner of the business is being *out
in the world* forming relationships with prospects and clients
and other owners of businesses, and the thing I feel time and
again is that those relationships are all about people; there's
still no substitute to sitting down face to face with someone and
having a good old conversation about what you're doing, what
you're all about, how you want to work as a business. That's still
fundamentally important.

I do think there were times when people were leaving us, that we
could have been more *generous and a better employer* ... whereas
we started out as well-regarded and well-liked. I think we came
to be thought of as sharp-elbowed and maybe a bit brutal.
Because we were so focused on the outside.

I think when you're doing a big scaled-up task, you *just don't know*
what you don't know, and you have to learn about processes
and structures the hard way.

I think so much of it is *luck* in terms of being at the right place
at the right time in these kind of happy coincidences that
happen – in terms of hitting the external market spot on
and then developing what you need to do to scale it up
organisationally.

I think because we've had so many different experiences together,
it gives us more *confidence and trust* to know that the next thing
that comes along – we'll be able to get over it. You know, when
you go through a very difficult thing with a group of people,
and then overcome adversity, it makes you even stronger for
the next thing you have to face. Setting up internal structures is
not so hard.

If I were to do something else now in terms of an
entrepreneurial business, I feel I know enough, and knowing
enough often means, 'No no, I want to hire those three
people from day one, because I know that *I've got those gaps
from day one.*' But most entrepreneurial leaders don't
realise this.

Part 3: Organisational Muscle Workout Practice – Moving from the Current State to the Future State

• Understand the current and necessary future state of this
  organisational muscle.
• Through this identify the organisational muscle to be
  developed.
• Put in PLACE a workout plan to develop the muscle – with
  milestones, targets and regular check-ins on whether the muscle
  is being developed.

As with the other workouts described, the first part of the process
is to understand where the organization is today so that, as an
organisation and as a leadership team, you understand where the
focus should be.

These are the seven key questions to ask yourself as an organisation as you look at the right balance of internal and external focus:

1. How much time does the leadership team spend looking
   at the external market? In your leadership meetings, how
   much time do you devote to external (customer-facing) issues and how much to internal issues and capability? How
   much leadership energy is consumed on external versus internal issues?
2. Who is accountable internally for the internal operations –
   that is, how do you ship your product or service? Does this
   person(s) sit on the leadership team? If yes, what role do they
   play? If no, do you have a gap on the leadership team?
3. What percentage of your staff is focused externally on the customer and on customer acquisition, and what percentage of

your staff is focused internally on delivering the product/service to the customer? Is this the right balance? Is it working?

4. Given how you currently do things, can you deliver 10× what you do today in the same time frame, with the same quality and at least the same cost structure (if not lower)? Will the processes, procedures and operating instructions for the organisation allow you to scale up to achieve this?

5. What does your current organisational structure look like – how are you configured today? Is this congruent with what you want to achieve? Does this configuration allow you to scale, or do you need to make changes as to how you are internally structured? Is this a sustainable organisation structure as you grow and scale?

6. Customer obsession: Is being obsessed with the customer a good thing? Are you only obsessed with the customer? And nothing else? Are you obsessed with delivering for the customer in a way that scales and grows your business? Do you offer different versions of your product or service? What are the internal costs of this differentiation in customer experience – is the cost trade-off worth it?

7. As an organisation it is important to know the internal cost of delivering to each of your customers. Some customers are clearly more valuable that others in terms of the top-line revenue number – but what is the internal cost of servicing those customers? You need to dig deep into the data. Whose role is it in the organisation – to be the person who looks at monitoring the organisational progress according to the metrics?

Having asked these questions of the organization, the next section gives seven key workouts that the organization can perform in order to develop the right muscle to address any gaps or issues raised by the answers to the key questions above.

Workout Plan

1. *Customer 360° Muscle Workout*
    Take your top 20/50/100 customers. Conduct a 360° view of each of those customers:

What is the revenue that each customer brings to the organization – today and projected next year?

What is the cost of servicing the customer – today and projected next year?

This gives you the profitability cost per customer – today and next year.Based on this information, build out a plan to service that customer, adding new resources as needed.

2. *Sharing Data Muscle Workout*
    Share the results (on an aggregated level) with all the employees across the organisation. Instil in each employee an understanding of revenue/cost trade-off per customer.

    Get the balance right between sharing aggregated data (no single customer identified) and driving actionable insights to help the organisation to service the customer in the most efficient and effective way possible.

3. *Reward Muscle Workout*
    Identify and analyse how employees in the business are rewarded. Map out for each employee how they are incentivised: base salary, benefits, bonus and stocks/shares. Based on this data, do you have the right reward structure in place to grow your business in a sustainable way?

    Identify which roles are rewarded for customer acquisition (without taking into account customer *cost* of acquisition or ongoing costs). Is this the best structure for your organisation? People behave in the way they are rewarded to behave. Ensure you are driving the right behaviours by rewarding the right behaviours.

4. *Connecting Muscle Workout*
    Identify the role in the organisation that is accountable for connecting the customer feedback from external sources to your product/service teams. How many of these roles do you have? Do you have enough of them? Does the accountable person for this role report directly to the CEO? They should.

5. *Processes/Procedures/Ways of Doing Things Workout*
    Map out all your customer-facing process, procedures and ways of doing things. This is not always the easiest job to do! If you do not have this mapped out, written down, how do you know whether all employees in the company are doing this?

Identify which processes over-deliver/under-deliver for the customer and what are the costs of each process/procedure. Identify the capability in the organisation to do this – if it does not exist, then you need to bring in this capability.

6.   *Strategic Customer Planning Muscle Workout*
Write down your current customer base – number of customers, current revenue, next year projected revenue and so on. Is this enough to scale up your organization over the next few years? Do you need to expand your base of customers? Does your product fit into a niche, or can you broaden your customer base?

Are you dependent on a couple of key customers? Identify your most profitable customer profile. Survey your customers with specific questions: How does your customer use your product? What are the other ways in which the product can be used?

7.   *Key Internal Relationship Muscle Workout*
Analyse the relationship between the revenue-generating leaders on the team and those tasked with delivering the product or service. Is the working relationship aligned? There will be tensions/discussions, but is the relationship positive for the *sustainable* growth of the organisation?

Conduct an employee survey between the two parts of the organisation. This will identify how well they are working together. This is always going to be a natural tension point in the organisation. That is the fact of running your business. Pay attention to developing the connection points between these two muscles so they are working in an integrated way.

Now you are ready for Workout 4. Your role as a founder in the start-up has moved on; you need to move with it. That job title at the start – it no longer makes sense. So where are the founding team going now? Can they cope? Let's move on to Workout 4.

4

Workout 4: Allowing for Role Evolution – from Lack of Role Clarity to Role Definition

- Workout to change goals and tasks and transition roles and behaviours
- Define organisational resources needed for the future
- Build more directed teams and navigate complexity

Part 1: Discussion of the Organisational Muscle to Be Developed

Often, a typical entrepreneurial start-up organisation journey beings with a business with a small number of employees. They can be counted on the fingers of one hand, or both at the most. There are several distinct advantages to this at this early stage. Given the small number of employees, there is a sense of clarity around what is the goal or the task of the organisation – it is noticeably unambiguous. Countless hours have no doubt already been spent at this stage by the founding entrepreneurial leadership team on this very subject. If the business is highly product-driven, by start-up time the founders will be clear on what the product is, and/or what the organisation would like it to be. Likewise, if it is a service-driven business, the small number of individuals at the helm will know about the service being provided. Clear direction is there at the start, thanks to the few people involved.

Thus, we can see in the creation of the typical start-up scenario that the number of roles to be performed in the organisation usually outweighs the number of employees. Therefore, the relatively small number of employees in the organisation often perform multiple roles. The modus operandi is that not only is there an organisational desire that they wear multiple hats, but it is also actually an organisational imperative that they do so! Given this state, employees often have more discretion over what they would *like to do*, rather than focusing on what *needs to be done*. Is this a problem? It can be. It may have already happened among the founding leadership team members – they do what they want to do, rather than what needs doing. Because they often wear multiple hats themselves, in terms of the roles they perform in the organisation, their roles can often be ill-defined. They just have a go at everything. If the most important task to do on a particular day is to lick envelopes, then the CEO might be the one licking the envelopes!

As the organisation grows and scales – especially from a role-evolution perspective – then two things begin to occur. At the organisational leadership level, roles need to be become more specialist and less generalised. The founding leader cannot be the chief strategy officer, the chief finance officer as well as the chief customer officer. The organisation needs to identify the organisational capability and muscle that each of the founding leaders brings to the organisation and more clearly define their roles and how this role contributes to the organisational success. Because these 'employees' are also the founders in the organisation, the Board can play an important part in this process. The Board (and investors) can have delicate conversations that steer founding leaders towards the more defined roles they will need to have as the start-up develops.

Also, often the founding leaders might not have the broad experience required for some specialist roles such as the chief finance officer – this can be an organisational muscle that the start-up currently doesn't have time for and lacks the appetite to develop – and thus they may need to augment the senior team at this stage. From an employee perspective, this can also have an impact on the roles that employees perform and the tasks they undertake. These often need to be more clearly defined, particularly as a more complex organisational topography is often emerging. This 'role definition' muscle is often one of the hardest to identify and hardest to execute – and beef up when needed.

There are a couple of reasons why this workout can be the hardest one to perform. From an organisational perspective, employees who are either part of the founding team or brought on board early in the scaling-up process are often expected to wear multiple hats. Role success at this stage is often defined by being able to multitask and cover several different bases simultaneously – and often the organisational energy and buzz comes from playing these multiple roles. As the organisation grows and scales, and it becomes more complex, individual employees often operate in an environment which requires less of this 'can do whatever' attitude. Now they need a more systematic approach to either continuing to further develop the product or service or expand the organisation into related areas. Employees who are good at the 'can do – all hands to the pump' approach are often shocked. Now, there suddenly emerges a need for a more structured way to ensure that the organisational task or goal is performed or reached – and they are not yet used to it. The organisation needs to focus less on what specific individuals would like to do and more on what the organisation needs them to do.

Additionally, as the business takes on more and more employees, what was often an ambiguous role/goal/task that could be verbally explained to someone now needs to be codified and more defined. The roles and tasks that employees perform in the organisation are now written down. It is a stepping stone to being scaled-up – but it is not popular with everyone, at least not at first.

The evolving roles played by entrepreneurial leaders can be a key part of their ability to transform start-ups into more long-term, viable enterprises. These may not be conventional or obvious and may be entirely different to the roles assumed by leaders in bigger corporate organisations. These role preferences need to be combined with those of others to make a winning formula; much of the success of an entrepreneurial leader relates to the nature of the collective – that is, the other roles played by other members of the team. Role clarity can also be a focus on tasks which need to be completed before the start-up can achieve the transition. It can be argued that it is important for these tasks to be achieved – and less important about who is achieving them. And arguably all the roles are significant in the outcome.

This leads to one of the more difficult challenges facing an entrepreneurial leadership team. Are the team (or more usually the Board) in a position to assess whether the founding leadership team is the right team to grow and scale the organisation? Are roles appropriately defined at the leadership team level? If so, are the capabilities of the leaders undertaking these roles appropriately assessed to understand any gaps in capability? If there are gaps in capability, how can these be addressed? Are they 'coachable' or 'non-coachable' gaps? Depending on the answers to these questions, this can lead to minor or major role evolution at the leadership team level. This is arguably one of the most important areas for the organisation to address as it moves from start-up to scale-up.

The roles mentioned in Board-level discussions include those of being the visible figurehead of the organisation, which might include providing inspiration, and being pushy with a sense of urgency; not trying to do everything but coordinating, delegating and empowering; negotiating the recruitment of talented people as resources who can play to their strengths; training and retaining these people; not trying to be a lone hero but realising that success depends on many people's efforts – and the possibility of team-working/collaborative leadership. Providing a decentralised structure can help, but there is a need to monitor what is happening, liaising with the rest of the team. This can involve diffusing tension – crisis-handling – and a lot of communicating. It is about managing small teams as well as large ones – and being flexible enough to move on from being the entrepreneurial leader to whatever is next. The role of setting up an HR function is especially significant in helping the organisation move to the next level through careful resource allocation. Meanwhile, the essential role of the entrepreneurial leader will keep changing – that is the nature of it. But overall, it is predominantly geared towards the bottom line and survival – and especially achieving the transition to a scaled-up business.

Many leaders talk about the importance of being the figurehead, the personification of the organisation. The role of founder gets the media coverage, but many realise this may not be the whole story. And several entrepreneurial leaders want to do everything and need to ring-fence their energies and focus on one direction, delegating tasks. Many entrepreneurial leaders see their role as managing stakeholders, coordinating the overall team running the business and managing small teams as well as large ones. But there is a need to get clearer on the roles as the business progresses.

In the next section, we will hear from some of the voices and experiences of entrepreneurial leaders who have addressed these challenges along the way. Ultimately, there is no one playbook that makes this process work for every organisation. In Part 3, we will explore some of the questions an organisation can ask itself to understand how it can develop this specific role-evolution and role-definition organisational muscle.

Part 2: Experiences of Entrepreneurial Leaders

In this section of the chapter, we will hear some of the voices of the entrepreneurial leaders as they grappled with role clarity and role definition in the organisation, while trying to assess the current organisational capabilities versus future needs in the organisations.

Still the Figurehead, the Leader and the Strategist

From the beginning I considered myself the leader of the company and of our group of founders. Of course, the *scale of responsibility has changed over time,* but I always thought it was important to be seen in a leader role so that my clients would take me seriously. I also like developing my team. Strategy is my main responsibility and what I enjoy doing the most.

I am the visionary; I see where we could go with the company, how the market is developing. I analyse how the world is changing and evaluate how we should relate to that. I often talk to our bigger clients to share the strategy we have for the company.

I am the lead consultant in every deal, and I like it that way. My personality has been described as loud and dominant, because I like to be in charge, *and I have to admit that I struggle letting go.* I might have let go a little, but not much.

I wanted to be the boss, so I moved into the top job from Day One and saw myself as the main business generator. To a certain extent I delegated some tasks to trusted subordinates. I was fairly hands-off with the staff since I was busy enough negotiating new deals, and that didn't really change.

I fulfil the role of supervisor. I keep tabs on the performance, assuring service quality, and that isn't changing very much. I see it as my role.

Every time I took the role of lead entrepreneur I was looking at ways to grow the business fast so that I could sell it. I still do this pretty much.

It very much is you in the limelight all the time. I'm just a figurehead. I'm the one that comes in and shakes hands. They are the people who do all the work. *We do tend to glorify founders, but they don't do it all.*

The media is heavily balanced towards the entrepreneur media, is heavily biased towards what I call heroes. Journalists ask about the entrepreneur as hero. I say no. Because what is a hero? The person didn't build a multibillion-dollar company on their own. I would prefer somebody who said, and I'm just trying to think who would say, 'Actually it's me and this army of people.'

There is an example of a founder who came up with the idea of the company, who brought in other C-suite members on equity and they didn't gel because they felt they were doing all the work and the founder was getting all the interviews and the media invitations. So that actually turned nasty, and the investors who believed in the founder insisted that the others leave.

Some people will say, 'He's a fantastic entrepreneur. He's a great entrepreneur.' I know a great entrepreneur. Would I say he's a great entrepreneurial leader? No. Because *other people built the company.* His success was based on the hard work of an army of people behind him who chose not to be visible, or didn't have a choice.

Being an Inspirational Leader

I'd say my role is getting the most out of the people around me – inspiring others to be excellent and to gain the most out of our people.

The role of a leader is to inspire people to follow towards whatever the goal is that the leader is trying to accomplish. *Influencing people* to perform at their best and to give their all to whatever the common goal is, I think it's at the heart of leadership.

I think a big part of the role of co-founder and CEO is inspiration. I want to inspire the people that come to work for us for selfish reasons and also because I think it will make those employees more productive, better to be with, better individuals who are better around other people, better at teamwork; they'll be more engaged.

I think it's a great thing if you can inspire people that come into the organisation to be leaders. *They don't come in as leaders, but they pop out being leaders.* When things grow then it's more about creating a culture of leadership rather than just using the individual leader.

You have to work through other people as a leader. I have to accept that it's never going to be 100 per cent the way I want to do it. Even if I think I'm the smartest person, I have to find a way to articulate an inspiring idea and leave enough room for it to become something else so people can support it.

I think entrepreneurs are ... 'reckless' is not the right word, but entrepreneurs are very, very pushy by their very nature. They have to push hard on something special. They have to *question conventional wisdom*. They have to be forceful, insurgents in a market, and this can be inspirational.

Still Passionate about the Products

I still consult with our clients (advise them about potential solutions we can provide). I'm really passionate about the technology; this was one of the reasons we started the company. We still like to be involved in the development of the projects, even though the business is scaling up.

My role has always been as the brains behind the operation, creating and developing our product, but I also helped and enjoyed promoting our product through public appearances and events, *so my role has evolved* in this way.

I started off just as a salesman operating more or less door to door, and then changed to being a manager with emphasis on

training and mindset-shifting, and developing a business based
on quality and international standards.

Beginning to Delegate

Sales, technical operations, hiring, project management – I
have now started to delegate some of those responsibilities at
different levels.

I lead the operations side of the business and see this as the most
important role for me, and delegate tasks as and when needed.

In the past I've brought in more experienced people to help run
the company, the Board and the finance side. The trouble is,
as a person I'm capable of doing lots of things and invariably
there's some things I do that'll take me longer or I can get
bogged down in – and I think the challenge there is about *not
doing too many roles and trying to delegate* around you.

Managing Teams

I think teams are important, because whether you're the
entrepreneur or leader you have to manage teams and you
need them in the business. I can influence the smaller groups.
As the company got bigger, I found that the process ended
up being a lot more about stakeholder management, and
at the same time dealing with members of the Board, your
investors and some of your principal customers. And then,
the rest of the time was really working with your senior teams,
doing all sorts of 1:1's and just making sure that the product
development or the product growth was being done. The
role of the leader of a start-up ends up being *much more about
management of the senior team.*

I think we did it at the right time – creating a management team.
What we didn't do at first was to make it sufficiently complete.
I think there was always, especially in the early stage of a scale-
up, the feeling that we need a C-suite.

Working with the Board

I don't think we ever did a good job of using the Board ... then
we got a new CEO. We just had our first Board meeting
recently and it was superb. And that was the first time I felt ... I
could really *feel the Board was going to be used* correctly.

We've got better at saying, 'Here are the parameters. If it's in this
range it's green. If it goes to this range it's orange. In this range

it's red.' And then every Board discussion from now on would
be, 'We might like it to do better, but currently it's at level
green. Now, moving on, we've got to make decisions today in
this meeting, because it's red.'

From Doing Everything to Doing Mentoring and Coaching

Of course, at the beginning I was just learning and I was doing
a bit of everything, and figuring out stuff. Thankfully I had
people with experience who guided me through it. Now that I
am more familiar and comfortable with the business, I like to
get more involved developing and coaching my people. And it
is different for each of my start-up companies since they are at
different stages towards scale-up and the development of the
roles of the people are varied.

At the beginning when we didn't have employees besides the
founding team, I was doing the frontline work, and *now I am in
charge of leading our team and I also mentor them* and assign them
to our projects.

I am a people manager, making sure that everybody is happy with
their job and that they are doing the right things. As the most
visionary person in the company, I need to inspire them.

I see my role as driven by a passion for what I'm doing – I can't
expect others to be driven by the same passion – such as my
employees – they won't have the same passion. But I have to
pass on my passion to my customer. My role has to be something
I'm expert at. I have to know what it's all about and have
expertise in it – so I must have passion first, then knowledge –
then I try to pass this on to my employees, perhaps mentor
them. This hasn't changed.

Many of the young leaders I know who are now scaling up
companies have gone through some kind of near burnout.
They've been rescued by mentors and coaches. They were
seeking somebody they can use as a sounding board, to help
them figure out how to do things, at least to help list out what
they might be doing wrong.

Coaching is something I consciously worked on; I think not
everybody does. Or not everybody would think that they need
to learn or that it can be worked on, but personally I *definitely
consciously made an effort to do that* over my career. When I
was going up the corporate ladder I was rather keen to do
the courses, read the books, that type of thing, and then as
my career changed towards start-ups then to founding my
own company, I've really invested in coaching, and then my
coaching journey has centred on leadership to a large extent,

on what does that mean and *how do you get to be confident as a leader* and what type of leader are you going to be.

Being the Monitor of the Progress of the Organisation

I get all the information on where we're heading, how much money we have, who's happy and who's not happy, what clients we have – I get all that information. It's not easy, but once you have all the information, it's much easier to make a decision.

How do you judge you're being successful? I mean, growth is, obviously, a metric. It depends on if it's more business-oriented or if it's more people-oriented. I think I would say in business if there's growth, if revenue's increasing, if you're hiring more people, this could be an indicator of success, especially if your customers are happy.

In some companies, the leader role is being the person who knows the industry inside out. There's the sector credibility. That's why you have a lot of the think tank companies; the founders have worked in finance at some point. They understand the ins and outs of the sectors. In some cases, the leader is a specialist in the field, has credibility – and hats off, this person knows what they're doing, and we should follow.

With the need for wealth and success, it's really about making sure you deliver the bacon, deliver the wealth creation for the individuals, whether it's in terms of equity or whether it's earnings as well as other deliverables; you measure milestones.

Definitely customers are your number one source of feedback, and customers will not lie. They will be 100 per cent truthful. So if you build something that is truly useful, you will receive very good feedback, which can be a real testament to what you've created. Internally, of course, that's slightly different and how you do that; hopefully, you've inspired all the team leaders you have and the leaders below you in your organisation will help you measure that.

Roles Keep Evolving

At the beginning I was the tech expert, then led the tech side, then focused on building the company and creating structures and opening offices and making sure office supplies were there, and now I'm mostly focused on strategy. We had a very flat structure before, until a year ago, and then we were hiring people who are experts and giving them leadership roles. Then

I stayed as tech leader for one particular business line only. But then a month ago we put in a manager to run that – so my role has kept evolving.

I was pretty focused on sales at the beginning; it's my greatest strength and something I am naturally good at, but now I'm learning and personally developing more as a leader and taking on different roles.

I have a personal challenge of doing too much, of just getting involved in everything, and *transitioning from being the one person doing everything* to finding a specific role in the team was a hard challenge because you've been doing so much of it all as you've seen growth.

As you transform yourself into a leader of that organisation, you start learning not to be that person. An analogy would be: there's a difference between winning an election and governing, right?

It's okay not to be strong in everything. You need to be consistent, helping your people to eventually accept their strengths and how they cover the weaknesses, and that forms your leadership.

As the leader of a start-up you have to *accept your failings*, and build up those elements where you're not so strong.

You have to remove yourself from the picture. Being an entrepreneur is dangerous because at some point in time you get this impression that it's you against the world. It's been lionised as a role. There are urban legends about individual wolves going out there. In reality, it is a conscious removal of yourself from the picture.

As the company grew, my level of activity changed … I didn't have to do so much. That was the real transition. You tend to find that individual teams have their own support, a gang of guys, and they build up their own mini-cultures.

The entrepreneurial leader can let go. And I basically had less impact on the wider business beyond that of intellectual business piece.

In my first company, every time I had to reduce my scope, it was *gut-wrenching*. You start off doing everything … but I set myself a goal that within one year, if my calendar has 40, maybe 50, hours, half of the activities that I was doing will be owned and executed by somebody else.

When doing customer calls, as a leader, my goal was that within 12 to 18 months, somebody else should be doing the customer calls. That does free up your calendar. Doesn't mean that you have leisure time. It just means that you're able to concentrate on certain things. You're able to do *rich contributions* rather than touch 40 different things in 40 hours.

Now that we have heard the voices of entrepreneurial leaders and how they have looked at not only their own role evolution but also the role evolution of the leadership team and other members of the organisation, let's look at some practical questions that an organisation can ask itself to understand its current state of role clarity – who is accountable in the organisation, who is responsible for what in the organisation and why this is an important organisational muscle for the organisation to develop and grow.

Part 3: Organisational Muscle Workout Practice – Moving from the Current State to the Future State

- Understand the current and necessary future state of this organisational muscle.
- Through this identify the organisational muscle to be developed.
- Put in place a workout plan to develop the muscle – with milestones, targets and regular check-ins on whether the muscle is being developed.

As with the other workouts described, the first part of the process is to understand where the organisation is today, so you know, as an organisation and as a leadership team, where you need to focus.

These are the seven key questions to ask yourself as an organisation as you look at how roles are evolving in the organisation. Are you strategically thinking about organisational role evolution, clarity and capability?

1. Do you have the right mix of leadership skills in your organisation? Are you clear on the exact role that each person on the executive leadership team performs? If so, have you taken an audit of the capability of the leadership team to ensure that you have the right skills and capability – not just for today but for the future?
2. What role does the Board play in the company? Do you feel you have a strong enough Board to challenge you as a

leadership team? How many insiders are on the Board, and what is the balance of insiders and external parties? Has the Board been involved in role-definition/role-fit discussions with each person on the leadership team?

3. How clearly are roles in the organisation defined? When you recruit a role into the organisation, are you clear about what this role will do in the organisation? As the organisation grows and scales and as the roles evolve and change, do you regularly update the job specifications and role definitions?

4. Are you clear about the measure of success in each role? Does each employee have goals set and reviewed on a regular basis? Do they have a discussion with their manager on a regular basis (at least weekly) to discuss how they are doing in terms of achieving their goals?

5. Managers play a key role in helping to grow and scale your organisation. Not only do they organise the work and delegate the tasks, but they also help each individual grow and develop, which ultimately helps the organisation to grow and develop. Research shows that 70 per cent of the engagement scores of employees is related to their experience with their managers. How can you ensure that your managers have the capability/skills to create an environment for your employees to be successful at their roles?

6. Critical role assessment: Do you know the most critical roles in the organisation? Are there some roles more critical in your organisation than others? What are they? Are there single points of failure in these critical roles? Do you conduct a regular exercise to understand the critical roles in the organisation?

7. What is your process for 'future-proofing' your organisational skills? How much of the hiring of employees is hiring for today, and how often do you hire for tomorrow? Do you regularly conduct a talent-mapping exercise to understand what are the tasks that need to be done in the organisation, and do you have the skills internally (both today and tomorrow) to achieve these organisational tasks and goals?

Having asked yourself and the leadership team these questions and answered them honestly, what is your workout plan to help you get from your current state of organisational muscle to your future state? Below are some workouts to help you achieve those plans.

Workout Plan

1. *Leadership Roles Workout*

    Can you ensure that every member of the executive leadership team has a written job role/description? This sounds obvious. But you need to be confident that all members of the executive leadership team know each other's job role. Could you as a leadership team discuss any areas of overlap/ grey areas? Ultimately, the CEO/Board will decide if there is any disagreement between the members. As the organisation grows and scales, ensuring that there is absolute clarity and total lack of ambiguity around roles and responsibilities among the leadership team is important. This clarity will be important for decision-making and responsibility. Any grey/ disputed area needs to be made clear as soon as it becomes evident. Otherwise, this sense of ambiguity (and possibly of chaos) can permeate throughout the organisation.

2. *Leadership Capability Workout*

    Once there is a clearly defined role that the executive leadership team performs in the organisation, an audit can be conducted to ensure that each leader has the required skills and capability to perform that role. The easy way here is to look back at what the person has done, look at what the organisation needs to do, and to look forward to seeing if the person is capable of performing the defined role. This can be an informal activity using a 360° feedback process (whereby each member of the leadership team, the Board and subordinates of that person give feedback on their skills/capabilities). This should be conducted regularly. A more formal approach might be that the person goes through the process of 're-interviewing' for their role with the organisation. Whichever approach is taken, it is important that the organisation performs an assessment of the capability of each member of the leadership team to perform their role.

3. *Organisational Role Definition Workout*

   Like the leadership role definition workout, it is also important to ensure that every role in the organisation has a description of what the key tasks of the role are. As each role is hired into the organisation, there should be a full job description of what the role involves, the reporting lines, the goals that need to be achieved and other requirements. As the organisation grows and scales, the role will evolve and change, and very often there is no regular process to update this. A regular update (at least once a year) to the job description should occur to ensure that there continues to be organisational and individual clarity on the role and the tasks associated with that role.

4. *Individual Role Success Workout*

   There is a need to ensure that every role has a clear measure of what success in that role looks like. Each role should have monthly/quarterly goals to be achieved, and these should be agreed and documented. There should be a discussion at the start of each quarter between the employee and the manager about the goals for that period of time, and a discussion at the end about the level of goal attainment. Regular check-ins to support the employee on achieving the goals is a way to ensure there is a joint success metric – the employee is responsible for achieving their goals, and being successful in the role, and the manager has a responsibility to create the context/environment for that success.

5. *Critical Role Assessment Workout*

   Like all muscles, there are some muscles that are absolutely needed more than others. A role segmentation exercise needs to be conducted in the organisation – with a division of the roles into A, B and C – in order of importance (there can be a need to be ruthless here).

   What percentage of your roles are in A, B and C? All these roles (like muscles) are required, but some are more vital than others.

   Conducting an exercise like this will help shape your organisational approach to how you hire, reward, develop and try to retain specific roles – and think about succession planning for the future.

6.   *Management Capability Workout*

This workout depends on the role of the managers. Are they experts in their field and so manage experts, or are they generalists whose role is to organise and delegate the work?

Regardless of which side of the coin, there is a need to ensure clarity about what the managers do in the organisation. If they are super-experts, then there is a requirement to hire experts and promote them to the role. If professional managers are wanted, then the task is to hire professional managers with previous experience (so they don't learn on the job in a different context).

This workout involves some trial and error and will likely depend on the experience of the leadership team. It might be a 'try before you buy' workout, but it must be tried and completed first, and then the management team can see if there is a need to invest more in developing this muscle – or not. Either way, the workout will be invaluable.

7.   *Future-Proofing the Organisation Workout*

The critical role assessment tends to focus on roles today, but what about the skills and capabilities which are needed for tomorrow?

The leadership team needs to spend time to understand that as the business grows and scales, there will be a need for more or less of some skills/capabilities (maybe they can be automated or outsourced) and a need to bring more of some other skills into the organisation. The first task is to identify the person in the organisation who will be responsible for this workforce planning, who will put in place a plan to bring more of this capability into the organisation. In tandem, it's a good idea to write down the plan of how 10 per cent of the tasks in the organisation can be automated in the next 12 months. This will free up precious resources to help bring more of the future-oriented skills needed into the organisation.

Having spent some time understanding how roles are defined in the organisation and what the measure of success of each role is today, you can then begin the process of future-proofing by exploring what roles you do not have today that you will need tomorrow, and what are the measures of success of these roles. As the organisation grows and scales, roles will grow, scale, change, adapt, evolve and morph. Ensuring that you define and measure the success of the role organisational muscle that plays a part in that success is an important aspect of your organisational growth journey.

5

Workout 5: Coping with Risk – from One Single Point of Failure to Juggling Several Products, Processes and People Issues – Understanding Systemic Risk

- Coping with and minimising risk
- Taking calculated bets and avoiding the black hole of endless analysis
- Seeing the big picture, understanding the implications down the line
- Weighing up pros and cons; lack of action is a decision

Part 1: Discussion of the Organisational Muscle to Be Developed

Setting up any new business is a risk. In deciding to establish, and attempt to grow and scale a start-up organisation, the founding leadership team has already put itself on the path of being more comfortable with risk than most.

This workout discusses the concept of risk in the organisation and specifically as it relates to developing the leadership muscle to understand, analyse, mitigate and ultimately be comfortable with a certain level of risk in the process of the evolution of the business.

Managing and coping with organisational risk is an inherent part of a business as it starts up and moves to the scaled-up mode. Risks always exist: the risk of making decision A coupled with the risk of not making decision A; or making decision B. At either end of the evolutionary spectrum, the nature of the risk differs. At the early stage of the start-up, there is one overriding risk – the concern that the business will fall at the first fence, will fail soon after or will fail to scale up beyond the start. Thus, there are several overriding risks which give rise to a number of key decisions that need to be undertaken by a small number of people. As the organisation grows, the number of risks tends to increase, but then the overriding risks may subside; however, as time passes these risks then are distributed amongst a larger number of people (which can have its own pros and cons).

There are several key challenges that organisations will face as they grow and scale the operation, which vary over time but need to be appreciated from the start.

At the beginning of the organisational journey, when the start-up is not usually particularly complex, typically involving one product or service and a relatively small number of employees, the risks are usually immediate, near-term, well known and well articulated. Financial provision – funding for the organisation – is usually the major risk at this time. Revenue streams from the product or service being developed have yet to come on board. There's an external risk posed at this stage – that the product or service needs to get some level of market traction. A way to think about the risk at this point in the organisational journey is to think about it in terms of internal and external risk. Internal risk is usually well known and understood (and more under control), while the external risk is less known, and likely poses more of an issue.

From an internal perspective, things are moving at speed and at pace. The energy and buzz of the newly set-up organisation is entirely focused on getting the product or service to market as quickly as possible. There are usually a small number of decision-makers (sometimes just one in certain situations), so decisions can be made quickly and it is possible to then move on to the next. One major advantage of this situation is the rapid speed of decision-making. There are fewer roadblocks. But on the flip side, in moving at this pace, with a limited amount of input, not all the data or viewpoints might be considered to make the optimal decision. This is a common type of organisational risk trade-off which an entrepreneurial leadership team makes at this stage.

Given the profile of technology-focused starts-ups in particular, there is a tendency to be more comfortable with not necessarily succeeding the first time around. Getting to market a test version, a beta service, or an 80 per cent working model of the product or service, can be acceptable at this stage. As discussed earlier, often this type of market strategy approach will deliberately launch a less-than-optimal product or service into the market and use an instant customer feedback loop to further develop, enhance and hone the product. A mantra at this stage can be 'The enemy of good is perfect'. Thus, the internal risk profile and appetite of the organisation can be established and codified into the organisational culture at this stage. Taking calculated risks, particularly at a pace, can often become part of the modus operandi of the company.

This is often further enhanced by the profile of the leader who established the organisation or joined the start-up at any early stage. By coming on board the business at this point they demonstrated their risk appetite – likely to be higher than those in a more established set-up. Often, these start-up leaders are attracted to this type of organisation and, as a result, may have more influence, impact and decision-making propensity than they necessarily can have in more established and bigger companies. Such leaders can feel stymied by the processes, procedures and decision-making protocols of larger organisations.

As the business evolves, the number of decisions that need to be made increases in size (and potentially in complexity) and the number of people involved in those decisions can get larger as well. One key advantage of this is that as the company hires more individuals, the plan is that more subject matter expertise is being brought into the company. This can bring broader and/or different perspectives to the decision-making processes related to risk and the risk profile. However, there is also a flip side to this. At this stage, somewhat ironically, each new hire or employee into the organisation brings significantly more risk into the company.

The key challenge here is that as the organisation gets more complex, the risk in the business becomes more complex as well. The risk is no longer understood by any one individual in the organisation. Creating the right ways of understanding, analysing, mitigating and controlling for these risks becomes an important organisational muscle to develop.

But this is not to say that all risk is negative. With risk comes success or failure – which cannot exist without it. The aim of the organisational muscle to be developed here is to be able to cope with and minimise the downside of risk, while at the same time to double down on the potential reward that comes as an outcome of a successful calculated risk.

From an external perspective, as the organisation grows and scales, it acquires new customers for its products and services. The organisation now becomes dependent on those customers for revenue, and thus is required to service those customers in a way that guarantees further revenue streams.

Ironically, this introduces additional internal risk to the organisation. The organisation needs to balance the need to retain current customers with acquiring new customers. Aspects of how the product and service will develop will now be influenced more by customer demands. Balancing the customer needs (external risk), both now and in the future, with the ability to service those customer needs (internal risk), both now and in the future, creates a risk/reward trade-off. This again adds to the complexity of the organisation as it grows and scales, and the organisation leadership needs to develop the muscle to understand how to balance those trade-offs. The organisation will have limited resources in terms of time, money as well as people. This again becomes part of the systematic risk to be encountered.

Overall, we can see the typical start-up organisation having certain risk dimensions – an internal single point of failure risk in a relatively un-complex environment, coupled with a product/service development focused on tactical, near-term customer needs. Additionally, there are limited internal decisions and decision–makers, which allows the organisation to move at speed and pace both in terms of getting the product to market and enhancing and developing the product based on external customer feedback. But this will soon change.

As the organisation scales up, the internal risk profile moves from a single point to systemic risk, and the internal operating environment becomes more complex. Additional hiring has brought on board people with different perspectives who no doubt have an opinion (or certainly would like to express an opinion) and be involved in decision-making. This can make decisions potentially more optimal but slow down the decision-making process. Along the way, more and more customers are providing rich data on how to develop, enhance or even change the product or service. The organisation cannot possibly prioritise all these requests, so now it has to take some calculated risks on how to strategically develop the product and service to retain as many customers as possible while also making the product and service marketable and scalable to a larger set of customers, in order for the organisation to grow and develop.

This movement along the risk continuum is the natural evolution of an organisation with a growth mindset. Now that we have identified and discussed this organisational muscle, the next section will hear from the experiences of entrepreneurial leaders around how they have navigated coping with risk, and the third section of this chapter will pose some questions on how to diagnose the current state of this muscle in your own organisation and then outline seven key workouts to help develop that organisational muscle.

Part 2: Experiences of Entrepreneurial Leaders – Managing and Being Comfortable with Risk

Below are some excerpts from our research interviews with entrepreneurial leaders and how they approached risk – how they analysed and managed their own and their organisation's risk appetite as they looked to grow and scale their organisations.

Measuring Risks

I have never been afraid of *taking risks*, but I would say that now I take *calculated risks*. Nowadays I evaluate if whatever I'm going to start is something I am passionate about, if I will have enough time for it and if it matches my life plan. Before now, I just entered unafraid without any kind of regard. Now as long as I can *measure it* and if I think I can *manage it*, I will take risks.

Offsetting Risks

We are not afraid of taking risk; we are often trying new products, and especially working in technology, we are *willing to try new things*. Also I feel at ease taking risks since I still have my full-time job in the background, so it's less risky than it could be.

Our founder had independent means, coming from a wealthy family, and would not be poor if the business failed, but it was *a bit risky at the start*, as a lot of time and effort were put into the business, although there were low barriers to entry.

Proving You Can Take Risks

I am not afraid of taking risks, I am more afraid of staying behind or being stuck. At the beginning, my family would have preferred that I took a safe, well-paid job, but I have proved that I can have my own business. I consider *myself resilient*, I have *failed in the past* but I'm not afraid of it anymore.

Our founder was a *risk-taker*. And the business was never completely stable, because the partners would come and go, customers would fluctuate, and negotiation with the local government produced variable results, so he never became complacent and always understood that risks would always be there.

Coping with Risk

For our founder, it was never so risky for him as he always had his main job to fall back on, but he realises that as the business is more scaled-up and more competitors are coming through, the risks associated with the business are increasing, but he has let go of responsibility with the appointment of the CEO, and the company is making alliances with other organisations, so a lot of the early-stage risk has disappeared.

Lots of young people working for us got incredible opportunities with us … And that's what a lot of them loved about it. I remember two or three people in their mid-20s being sent to become country managers. And they did it really well, coping with such a fast-growth environment.

Our *risk attitude* was very high at the start – especially as everyone was against our founder. People didn't believe in us – then eventually we could contain risk with higher quality – but risk was always there – especially in our particular business.

Yes, I just had to come to terms with the fact that *risk is unavoidable*. I have learned to cope with it; I now see it as experimentation rather than risk now. I understand that I will get something out of it – it could be a new product, or *when it fails I still get new knowledge*.

With experience I have learned how to take risk, but at the beginning it was *difficult to take risks* and quite scary.

So in the beginning of any company it's a little bit like the Wild West. Everybody makes decisions. 'Okay, they made a mistake, oh well.' Everybody's going so fast that the expectation of it being without risk is laughable. *Everything has risk associated with it*, so, you know, bad things happen and you just keep moving on. But it's not seen as a mistake really, it's just seen as a natural evolution of a company, kind of finding its feet within a market – it happens.

Creating a Risk Profile

It has changed over time. We even have posters on our walls that say 'Screw it, lets do it'. If we believe something will work for us we just go ahead with it. We don't do that much of market research or competitor analysis; we just do it because we believe that by doing you learn the most.

The *attitude change at a specific moment in time* for the company, when you're able to say no to clients, when the influx of projects is larger than the capacity you have, then you can start making choices – you can analyse the risk then.

Are we earning money, or does this project sound interesting for us? We normally go for the latter; we like taking risk rather than doing boring projects. The proportion is *80 per cent risky, 20 per cent safe projects*. When people look at us they consider us a company that takes risks.

In *larger organisations,* I think there's the luxury of having
a history in terms of understanding exactly what type of
leader might succeed or fail in a given environment. *There's
a perceived greater level of certainty* that you can succeed,
whatever that expected value of the future contribution.
There's perceived certainty about that and people are
quicker to move, and make different decisions in terms of
whether a leader is a good fit or not, but there needs to
be a huge appetite for risk in a start-up because there's so
much unknown. Often the people making the decisions are
themselves at the same level of experience as the others and
take risk upon themselves, so that combined experience set
(or lack of experience set), I think, leads to an environment
where people are taking risks all the time, because a lot of
people inevitably don't know what they are doing.

Wanting to Take the Risk

You're not happy when people say no, so people like us
(entrepreneurs), we are getting used to being criticised. We are
getting used to being said no to us, of people saying no to you.
When people say yes to you, we really appreciate it. I mean, why
should people say yes to you? You have to prove yourself. We *are
keen to take the risk* then.

Our founder says he is risk-prone, he tries to be more calculated.
But he assures us that he actually *thrives on chaos and can cope
with risks.*

I have always been *comfortable with risk.* It's just that now I am more
experienced and know how to evaluate the risks better, and
I'm not afraid of them. It is a skill that matures with you, in
practice.

I've always been a *risk-taker,* I always wanted to do more than just
be an employee, I wanted to realise my dreams, I wanted the
excitement of doing my own thing. I still take risks every day, I
like it that way. Ours is a tough business. You are only as good
as your last project. But I thrive in this environment.

Evolution of Risk-Taking

There was definitely *more risk at the beginning of our business;* the
impact of what we do is less risky now – there's a much smaller
risk now. We know now that we can start a business and scale it
up, and we are spreading our risk around now. We are not risk-
averse now, but we are certainly less keen on risk than we were
four years ago.

Having a family changed my *attitude towards risk*, but when I think they are OK and provided for, I just go back to how I was when I was 20. So my attitude towards risk is really just the same as it has always been.

At the beginning I was more afraid of it, but with time your decisions start becoming clearer; at the beginning you *are full-on gambling*, after some time you get a better sense of it. Nowadays I don't like to ponder for long. I make a point of setting myself a time limit to make a decision.

It used to be *really stressful*; now I'm used to risk. I know that it's about handling the stress – I just live with it. It is part of the deal, I just get on with it.

I think one of the problems with start-up businesses is that you normally recruit junior and inexperienced people because you're never brave enough to recruit expensive people who've got ability and who can work with you at the same level, so you are constantly having to nurture and advise and manage, and it is incredibly stressful. *More experienced people can take risks*, but the less experienced don't really know what to do.

I found as I started to recruit more experienced engineers and more qualified people, *they took the responsibility* and it became just so much easier to manage organisational growth, with less risk, and my leadership style as founder became more about communicating and working through the problem together, rather than telling them what to do all the time.

I think the *ability to cope with risk* depends on how quickly the organisation is growing. I think it happens relatively quickly, at different times, for different leaders in the same organisation. As you build out the business you will be changing leaders because they have different skill sets, and they also like the job better when it's smaller or they like it when it's bigger. And it's a little bit of a timing issue – when's the right time to do that?

Part 3: Organisational Muscle Workout Practice – Moving from the Current State to the Future State

- Understand the current and necessary future state of this organisational muscle.
- Through this identify the organisational muscle to be developed.
- Put in place a workout plan to develop the muscle – with milestones, targets and regular check-ins on whether the muscle is being developed.

As per usual, the first part of this section is to diagnose the current state of the organisational muscle – in this workout as it relates to risk – and then put in place a series of workouts to further develop that muscle.

These are the seven key questions to ask yourself to diagnose the current state of your organisational muscle:

1. Internal risk: Do you know what your top 10 internal risks are in the organisation? Are they product/service risks, process risks or people risks? Have you conducted an internal audit of your most important processes (ways of doing things) to ensure they are fit for purpose and scalable?
2. External risk: How much time do you spend on market intelligence? Where do you get your market intelligence from? Is there a specific person in the organisation whose role is to synthesise all the external market intelligence?
3. Customer risk: When was the last time you conducted a segmentation of your customer base? How do you know which customers are the profitable ones? Which ones have the most potential for growth? Which ones cost you the most money to service?
4. People risk: Are there single points of failure in your organisation? What are the critical roles in the organisation that – if the person either leaves the organisation or does not perform their role – could have a potential negative impact on your organisation? For roles that are single points of failure (only one person does or knows the job), what is your plan to ensure that you have an alternative or a successor for that role?
5. Leadership/Board discussion: How often as a leadership team do you take a critical look at the risks in your organisation – both current and future? How much time do you devote to risk discussion at your executive leadership/Board meetings?
6. Risk appetite: Do you know what your individual and leadership risk appetite is? Do your employees know what this is? How much do you talk about risk, taking risk, calculated risks? Is this the same for every part of your organisation? Remember that your organisational risk appetite will evolve over time, just as your culture evolves over time. How do you

know that your actual risk appetite as an organisation matches the actual risk appetite that is practised in the organisation?

7. Risk/reward time horizon: As your organisation moves from start-up to scale-up, the time horizon begins to shift from just having immediate, short-term tactical risk (and potential reward) to having both the short-term and the longer-term strategic risk (and reward). Balancing both risk elements can be challenging, as sometimes they are not always aligned or can even be in direct conflict. How often do you consciously weigh up the short-term risk/reward versus the long-term risk/reward?

Having now asked yourself and the organisation those seven key questions, let us now focus on the seven key workouts that can develop the organisational muscle relating to risk as an outcome of the organisational enquiry.

Workout Plan

1. *Internal Risk Analysis Workout*
    Strengths and weaknesses (SW): what are the strengths and weaknesses in your organisation? Focus on the three Ps: your product (or service), people and a process perspective. Are there single points of failure in your organisation? What are your top 10 weaknesses that you should address? Write these down, and these become part of your organisational objectives for the next 6–12 months.

2. *External Risk Analysis Workout*
    Opportunities and threats (OT): What are the opportunities and threats external to your organisation? Put the threats into three separate buckets: those you can control, influence and cannot control. Ignore the ones you cannot control and take the top 10 from what you can control or influence and use this to inform part of your organisation plan for the next 12 months.

3. *People Risk Analysis Workout*
    Write down the names of the top 20 per cent of the critical roles/people in your organisation. They are critical because if they left your organisation tomorrow it would pose a

substantial risk to your business being able to scale and grow. Write down a plan for each of those employees to retain them. Then take the next 30 per cent of your start-up from a role/ people perspective. Write down a plan for each of them to become a successor to the top 20 per cent of your organisation. Ensure you have at least one viable internal successor for each of the critical roles you have identified. If you don't have a viable internal successor, you need to hire one.

4. *Delegated Risk Workout*
    As an entrepreneurial leadership team, you cannot manage every risk in the organisation. As you hire employees into the organisation, ensure you are delegating risk (otherwise known as responsibility) to those individuals. Otherwise, there is a chance of creating risk/decision-making bottlenecks in the organisation. No one person can understand all the risks in a business, so delegate the risk and ask the manager/leader of a particular area to identify the risk/responsibilities in their area and then take ownership to put in place a plan to eliminate or mitigate that risk.

5. *'Match Your Risk Appetite with Your Culture' Workout*
    Managing culture is an extraordinarily strong entrepreneurial leadership muscle to develop (this will be discussed in more detail in Workout 6). As part of your risk appetite, look to see how your culture views/thinks about risk. Identify the language that you (and your leadership team) use around risk in the organisation. Does the language give carte blanche to all employees to take risks, or do they understand where to take risks and where not to take risks?

    Identify ten employees in your company and chat to them about risk and what they think the risk profile and appetite of the organisation is. If it matches your hoped-for view – then you have done a great job; if not – then you know what action you need to take! Ensure your culture of risk appetite matches your actual risk appetite.

6. *Risk Discussion Workout*
    Ensure that you discuss organisational risks at least once per quarter at the executive team leader/Board level. The rigour of doing this will help in several ways. It will elevate risk and make discussion of risk part of your organisational way of

doing things. Not every risk is equal; trying to understand the impact of risk before something happens helps you to plan for what resources you need to tackle it now – or if you do not tackle it now, what resources will you need to tackle it when it happens? Discussing risk regularly is an important part of coping with and understanding risk.

7. *Risk/Reward Time Horizon Workout*

Consciously spend time trading off the short-term risk/reward versus the long-term risk/reward. To make it to tomorrow, you must survive today. Operating in survival mode can mean that longer-term issues are stored up for later, so the organisation needs to have a plan to move from surviving to thriving. Decide on three things each quarter that will move you from survive to thrive mode. It could be more access to funding, more employees, more revenues – have a clear plan to move your risk time horizon from the short term to the longer term. By exercising this muscle you will get there!

6

Workout 6: Managing Culture Change – Understanding Person– Culture Fit from an Additive Start- Up to Matching the Values of a Sustainable Business

- Working to build the desired culture
- Moving from culture 'fit' to culture 'additive' – to absorb new cultures, not to reject but to integrate
- Moving from a start-up culture and (lack of) structure to a sustainable operation – but keeping the start-up vision and values

Part 1: Discussion of the Organisational Muscle to Be Developed

As the entrepreneurial leadership team strives to move the start-up business to a more scaled-up mode, one of the trickier areas to scale and develop is the 'culture' of the organisation. Culture in the organisation is akin to goodwill on the company balance sheet: extremely hard to accurately measure and very subjective, and often its value is not entirely understood – that is, often until a situation may arise that it turns from a positive to a negative force in the organisation. Then it can be blamed for all sorts of problems – again, without real understanding.

Thus, defining the concept of 'culture' is a very subjective process. For the purposes of this book, we will view culture as 'how we do things around here' – how you hire people (the process, the approach, the philosophy), how you let people go from the organisation, how you make decisions, how you prioritise, how you plan out the office, what approach you take to product development, how you view quality and its measures, how you treat your customers, how you price your product or service – all of the hundreds and thousands of actions, activities and outcomes that happen in any organisation on a daily, weekly and monthly basis. All of them set a tone for what the culture of the organisation is – how a decision is made tomorrow is influenced by how a similar decision was reached yesterday – it is 'the way we do things around here'.

In growing a company from a start-up venture to a more mature scaled-up organisation, it must thus be emphasised that culture plays an important part in the definition of 'how we do things around here'. One of the more philosophical ways to think about scaling an organisation is that – in essence – what an entrepreneurial leadership is doing is trying to simply scale a culture, scaling an organisational 'mindset' around how things get done in this particular context.

What the entrepreneurial leadership team is attempting to do in the process of scaling up is to try to translate the organisational vision for their product and service into a hundred, a thousand or a million different actions that will help realise that vision. A key component to realising that vision is ensuring that the organisation has the right culture, the right 'way of doing things' to help execute that organisational vision – and make it a reality.

This involves scaling a mindset, scaling a specific approach about how an organisation does everything from identifying customer problems to delivering the products/services to meet customer needs and – in between that – ensuring that the organisation and the leadership team are able to balance all the internal and external resources and requirements to help ensure that 'the way we do things around here' is scaled up for the future.

Focus on Culture

Looking at organisations which have effectively moved from start-up to scaled-up mode, a major driver behind this is the process of moving the organisational culture to a new level.

Some start-ups, at the very outset of their organisational journey, make a very conscious decision to focus on what the culture of the organisation will be and spend significant organisational time and energy to setting the right tone, the right atmosphere, the right way of doing things (as the organisation views it). Often, this process will start with the initial founding leadership team. They will often come together as a leadership team because they share similar values, views and 'ways of doing things' that make them want to start a company together in the first place. That is not to say that they are all similar, but that they often share a similar philosophical approach – either through identifying customer problems, identifying gaps in the product market or service, or simply that they do not want to work for a larger, more corporate (in their view) organisation. And they are looking for a new way of operating which is more satisfying, involves less compromise on their part and offers potentially more rewards, in either monetary or non-monetary terms.

For organisations which are consciously doing this exercise of focusing on culture, often, as a first stage in the process, they either write a company mission statement (what they want to achieve), decide on a set of company values (how they want to behave, operate and get things done) or formulate an organisational vision (what the outcome and impact of the organisation will be). Or all three. These can often be codified and written down, thus becoming the organisational 'handbook' or reference guide for 'how we do things around here' – and especially used for new recruits to guide them into understanding 'how things work around here'.

On the flip side, some organisations do not necessarily spend the same amount of organisational energy and bandwidth on formalising this culture into a written statement, but whether they do this or not, the organisation culture, the 'way we do things around here', will emerge – whether they like it or not. It is a living organism which can take on a variety of forms.

This initial founding leadership team, then, whether consciously or unconsciously, sets the tone for what the culture of the organisation will be. They do this in the words they speak, the documents they write and the way in which they behave, with themselves and their organisations. Thus, the leadership team in any organisation, but particularly in a start-up, sets the tone of expectations by how to speak, act and behave. Other employees look to them for signals around what success looks like for individuals in this organisational context and environment. Thus, these leaders' actions are magnified, both positively and negatively, by other employees in the organisation. You don't have to look too far to see how the behaviour of the leaders of a start-up can positively or negatively impact the organisation. Thus, leadership behaviours can have profound effects on the norms and rules of 'how we do things around here'. And, of course, there can be two cultures at least: the one which the leadership team wants to create and a second culture or subculture which naturally evolves, beneath the surface – the 'real' culture which the employees drive as a reaction to the leadership team.

Cultural Evolution

As the organisation grows and scales, a very tangible aspect of this is hiring new employees into the set-up, especially as it continues to evolve. As the organisation grows, the current 'culture' begins to morph and change in a greater or lesser degree as each new employee comes on board. Each new employee who joins the organisation will bring an additional piece to the tapestry of the culture within the business and help in its evolution. As the organisation develops and grows its organisational capability and muscle (through each new employee), the new individual coming on board brings not just their talent and capability but also their own way of doing things.

This is particularly noticeable if the organisation hires employees who have previous experience in other companies. These employees will usually have had experiences in other cultures and have seen other ways of doing things – and have got used to these. Often, the success of employees hired into the organisation as it grows is to ensure that they can be successful in the new culture. However, on the flip side of this, the culture is not static; it is very much a dynamic process that is ebbing, flowing and evolving every day within the organisation, especially with the ups and downs of its performance.

Thus, as the organisation hires more employees into the company, they can have an influence on its evolution. This can be observed especially as the start-up hires more leaders or managers into the business. Many start-ups experience a culture which undergoes rapid change, either in the culture direction or in the pace of change within the culture, as the organisation brings more senior employees into the business. We will speak more about this in the next part of the chapter.

Likewise, cultural change and evolution can be forced upon the organisation, particularly within those that are bringing a new product or service to market. The customer feedback loop brings additional data points into the business thinking and thus can impact on 'how we do things around here'.

This is very noticeable in organisations that bring pilot or beta products to the market. They are actively seeking feedback from the customer on the appropriateness and effectiveness of the product or service to meet the customer needs, the quality of the product that is in demand and, in some cases, what the customer would like to see in version 2.0 or version 3.0 of the product.

Thus, unless the organisation is standing still (which is exceptionally unlikely in an organisation that is looking to scale and grow), each piece of growth – whether that is a new employee, feedback from a customer on the product, a decision made on a product feature or market landscape – will bring cultural change and cultural evolution to the organisation. This dynamic process of cultural change is a hard one for the organisation to fully control or have 100 per cent influence over. Total control of culture change is impossible – but it can be influenced and to a large degree managed.

Culture Fit versus Culture Additive

One of the ways in which an organisation can attempt to manage this cultural evolution is by controlling the levers that bring about this culture change. As discussed previously, one of the most tangible aspects of this is the hiring of new employees into the company. As the leadership team hires new people, they tend to look to see if these new employees 'fit' the existing culture of the business. They can do this in a rigorous way by extensive interviewing, profiling, personality- or assessment-testing, and competency-based questioning. Often, the interviewers are looking for signs to ensure that each new employee 'fits' into the culture of the organisation – how they tend to do things – and this is how the company tends to want them to do things. However, this approach needs to be treated with some caution. Culture 'fit' can often be a code word for excluding people who are 'not like us'. This can then tend to veer into the area of bias (either conscious or unconscious) and have implications for the diversity and inclusiveness of the organisation. This can often be explained by levels of satisfaction with current employees and/or the leadership team being happy with the status quo of 'how we do things around here' and not wanting things to change. However, the reality for the organisation to grow and scale up is that 'how we do things around here' will need to change on a very regular basis! How the organisation operated to win the first customer, or deliver the first version of the product, is unlikely to be a successful way to win the 100th customer or deliver the 100th version of the product.

The irony here is that if the company only hires people who 'fit our culture', this could have a detrimental effect on the likely success of growing and scaling the company. As the business looks to hire more employees, they should instead explore whether the person is 'culture additive' to the organisation. In simple terms, this concept means that the newly hired culture-additive person may generally do things the way the organisation does things (so they can quickly be successful in the cultural context of the organisation), but some aspects of how they do things might differ (so they bring a new perspective to the organisation to help in the process of adapting, evolving, changing and growing). In this sense, what the 'culture-additive' new hire is bringing to the organisation is 'new ways of doing things' which will add new cultural elements to the organisation. If the new employee is a senior member leader in the organisation, this 'new way of doing things' can become part of the established 'how we do things around here' and the culture begins to evolve and change, with the newly added features, in an easily digested way.

Likewise, the new person hired could be consciously brought into the organisation to develop new cultural 'muscle' – to deliberately bring new ideas/fresh ways of doing things. Thus, whether it is conscious or unconscious, an organisation's culture beings to evolve and adapt as each new employee joins it. The challenge for the company is, how much do we want the culture to be flexible and additive to new ways of doing things? Or, how much rigour does the current leadership team demand of the current culture, to be reinforced and more stable?

Again, there is no one way of doing this – just being consciously aware that whether or not an organisation decides to do something about the evolving culture, it will develop by itself. Like an adolescent child growing into adulthood, an organisation – if it wants to scale and grow – will embark on a similar journey. There are aspects of the development that the leadership team can influence and manage, but there are also aspects of this process over which they will have much less control.

Thus, building the organisational culture muscle needs sensitivity to what is needed, but it must also allow for elements of organic development at the same time. The leadership team needs to reinforce the culture – but they must also realise that they cannot control it completely, and that natural evolution will always happen.

Approaching the scaling of the organisation with the mindset that this will involve the scaling of the culture is a positive way to frame how to think about this. For the organisation to grow and scale, it will inevitably need to change and evolve. For the culture to support this growth, the organisation cannot (and anyhow will not!) stay static; it will evolve, change and morph as well. Looking at this organisational cultural change as a dynamic driver of the organisation growing and scaling is a helpful way for it to learn to 'let go' and not stay bound to 'how we do things around here'. It is a necessary and important part of the organisational growth process. It also has incredibly positive impacts in terms of creating as diverse and inclusive an environment as possible in an organisation. This is not just the right business thing to do; it also happens to be just the right thing to do!

Having explored the concepts around developing the organisational cultural muscle, in the next section, we shall hear from the voices of entrepreneurial leaders on their experiences surrounding organisational culture and cultural change as they started up and scaled up their own organisations.

Part 2: Experiences of Entrepreneurial Leaders – Managing Culture and Cultural Change

Flat Structures Define a Culture Type

> I like people with lots of creativity, who care about what we are doing. As a knowledge-based company, we are mostly professionals, so we are more flexible and flat in structure, and *this defines our culture.*

> We are not hierarchical at all; we are like a web, and we are all connected. I trust my team and I feel supported by them and I am there for them too. It's a relaxed, flexible culture.

> We are *flat and flexible,* with almost no hierarchy, as long as deadlines and objectives are met. We don't have an organisational structure, it's very flat. Resources are shared, and the partners serve as heads of certain departments or areas of the business.

> As founders we are more flexible, we split responsibilities. For our employees we give *as much freedom as possible,* but we work based on goals and objectives; we keep track of key performance indicators. In a flat structure, there are not many layers besides founders and employees.

> We have a huge portfolio of subcontractors; they are not really employees, and we find experts in different industries. They do not have a hierarchy because there are not many layers, but our management team (especially the founder) is the head of the business.

Not All Start-Ups Are Flat

> *Hierarchy* is necessary for our type of company. We have a big group of operational people who need a supervisor, so we are far from being a flat structure, so our culture is more *traditional.*

The hierarchical culture is actually what we really need. This kind of structure is required for the business to run correctly; *employees need lots of supervision.*

Our culture is still entrepreneurial but is becoming more market-driven with the establishment of our brands and feedback from customers – and having a bit more of a mature structure in the business.

Staying Entrepreneurial

We were a bit clannish to start with, but under the direction of the founder we became much more entrepreneurial, and more or less stayed that way, as he did not implement enough processes and policies for it to become bureaucratic – although that was to happen after he was pushed out by a gang of more ambitious colleagues who wanted us to be more formalised and 'professional'. As a start-up, we are flat, have mostly young people, and are flexible.

We are entrepreneurial – I like working with knowledgeable business people, I still have a lot to learn. We are market-driven but still entrepreneurial. I want to build a clan culture, but people come and go too much. *There is not a lot of loyalty here,* this business is very opportunistic.

Even Start-Ups Have a Mix of Cultures

Our culture started off as very entrepreneurial; we're trying to keep it that way. Our company started up in a start-up incubator – but we are becoming more market-oriented with the *pressure to produce a financially viable product.* We are realising that our culture is changing – but we are leaving the issues of being more market-oriented to the commercial guys so that we can keep our culture of innovation in our product-development area.

Family-Oriented Even If Not a Family

We have an informal, very young team (average age 29) and a management team (33). Not a family business, but people have quickly become friends. Something I like is that people who have left our company often come back to say hi and stay in contact. We are also ambitious, but we are not arrogant, we don't brag, but *we deliver what we promise.* It was very entrepreneurial at first, but has settled down to being a bit clannish with some of our new people; they are now a bit of a happy family.

Cultures Evolving

We still want to have a start-up mindset, but at the same time we want the dynamics of a corporate. A few years back we were trying to keep the entrepreneurial style – at the start people in the company were switching hats all the time, but now we are more structured – maybe a bit more market-oriented.

I suppose the culture of my businesses does change over time; normally they start being very disorganised but then *they get more organised over time.* If the business grows bigger, I bring in other people. I don't have qualifications – they might have MBAs – I don't – then I'm redundant – this is OK by me.

Trying to Keep the Values

We believe in championing small business; we believe that a strong sense of *shared values* enables us to maintain a common company culture and community, no matter how large we grow. Our customers come first, then employees second and shareholders third.

Our team is being integrated by passionate go-getters with a lot of grit. Our founder favours the start-up culture, but he compromised on people – not everyone is like this.

If you look at the biggest start-ups now or the little scale-ups, culture has very much come from the founders. And *I think it's not a burden.* It is very important, one of the most important things, that from the start, you establish a culture that, obviously, you want to establish. So, what are your values? What's the purpose? What is the mission?

The first role for many entrepreneurial leaders is an obsession of making our customers successful. I know every company says that, every entrepreneur aspires to that. I haven't yet met an entrepreneur or company that says, 'I don't want my customers to succeed.' But making that as the lynchpin of every discussion, making that a lynchpin of every all-hands meeting – of course, your first all-hands meeting is you and your co-founder – there is no need to emphasise customer obsession in a large setting, but we did. That became *the biggest tool for influence* because I wasn't prepared how people would pit that philosophy, and it would manifest in many different ways, but it's key to success and a core value.

I've built into the business from day one really some of the *key concepts in terms of setting the right culture,* which are about transparency of what the business is doing.

We must have a clear vision and we must have clear values, and we must transmit them to the staff. And obviously I feel that's important as the owner of a small business of 25 people, and the peer group of owners I encounter in small businesses whom I talk to equally say that that is *critical to the success of their business.* I've been actively seeking out owners and co-founders of businesses who have passed the start-up stage and are looking to grow their businesses or have successfully grown their businesses, because that's exactly where I'm at – and they agree.

Driving the Culture

One of the things I enjoy doing is having a Monday morning meeting across the whole business. And I think that's helped me a lot and I like to *share and teach.* And I've made an impact on a lot of people here by talking about your financial health, your mental health. Things I enjoyed learning and reading myself anyway. I think that's something that's *shaped the culture and business over time.*

To me the culture is very important, because I realised they all needed to know how we came about ... it's certainly the culture of problem-solving, the culture of making a difference in people's lives in terms of what we build as a product ... this was quite a driving force.

The people in the business need to see the business operating in a way that's consistent with the flagship messages from the leaders, and that is something that has to be real and it has to be physical, and it has to be a continuing part of the operation of the business, and it has to be something that the leaders of the business actually model in person. And unless you're doing all of those things all the time, *you haven't got culture,* what you've got is a poster on the wall that nobody is really paying any attention to.

I want to know how I get from 25 to 50 to 100 people with the relative size of the business. I've had a few conversations with other people who are at the kind of 80–90–100-person stage, and what really struck me is how consistently those people talk about the importance of *setting the culture of the business* and communicating that relentlessly and in the right way.

Comparison with Big Business

> My sense about big business is they just completely fail to execute culture properly; they don't really understand it as an essential thing. In my experience, seeing it in big businesses, you'll get the director of HR on the Board saying, 'We really need to invest in culture,' and you'll get that big budget signed off or maybe a couple of million quid or something, and then they'll go to an agency and they'll create a beautiful, slick video and a slogan, and then try and push it through the organisation. *That's not like a start-up.*

> Why do attempts to deliberately build a culture in big business tend to just collapse? It's because the ability to execute successfully is different and big organisations don't know how to do it. They don't know how to train the right people to communicate the message, and they don't really understand how much work it takes to really get someone engaged with that type of messaging – that it's not just a poster on a wall, it's not just sending people for two hours to a study room to go through some kind of exercise once a quarter. To be *real and meaningful* for people, it must become part of daily life and it must be communicated well. And I think it is difficult to do that. Some smaller businesses can be more effective here.

Part 3: Organisational Muscle Workout Practice – Moving from the Current State to the Future State

- Understand the current and necessary future state of this organisational muscle.
- Through this identify the organisational muscle to be developed.
- Put in place a workout plan to develop the muscle – with milestones, targets and regular check-ins on whether the muscle is being developed.

These are the seven key questions to ask yourself to diagnose the current state of your organisational culture muscle:

1. Culture defined: How defined is your organisational culture? Do you have a mission statement as an organisation? Do you have stated and articulated organisational values? Did you

spend time as a founding leadership team to map out what type of culture you want to have in the organisation? How did you define this, and how did you codify this into your organisation? If you did not spend time as an organisation doing this at the start of the organisational journey, have you spent time since looking at the evolving culture?

2. Decision-making: How do decisions get made in the organisation? Are decisions made by the leadership team and then cascaded down to the lower levels of the organisation? How involved are employees in the decision-making? Are decisions made at the top of the organisation or are they made by consensus? Are people clear about who is the decision-maker for a particular process?

3. Diversity, equality and inclusion: Do you know the make-up of your organisation? What is the typical profile of people? What is the ratio of men to women? What is the percentage of people in your organisation from under-represented minorities? When you look around the leadership team and your organisation, do you see the diversity of your customers (both current and future) reflected in the diversity of the people in your organisation?

4. Hiring practices: Do you have a defined hiring practice for your organisation? What is the process for mapping out the hiring of a role? Who is involved in the hiring process? Are they trained in what to look for? Does someone have a veto on hiring a person into the organisation?

5. Culture language: What type of language is used by people in the organisation to describe the culture? Does it reflect the way you want people to act in the organisation? Does the language chime in a similar way for everyone? Does this language support what you want to achieve as an organisation and, more importantly, how you want to achieve it?

6. On-boarding process: What is the process you use to onboard people into the organisation? Is there a defined plan to set people up for success? How do you know whether they will be successful in your company? Are the responsibilities for this person well- or loosely defined? Does everyone in the organisation know what they are accountable and responsible for? When they joined, did everyone in the

organisation know what they are accountable and responsible for?

7. The 'acid test' of your culture: Do you have a 'brilliant asshole' in your organisation? A person who, through their skill set, experience or capabilities, has played a key role in taking your organisation from a start-up to where it is today, yet there are aspects to their behaviour that other people have complained about? Is there 'extra tolerance' of somebody in your organisation because they are good at their job but are perhaps really annoying to work with? Is this really 'culture additive' to your organisation?

Workout Plan

1. *Decision–Making Workout*
   Identify the top 20 decisions that need to be made in your organisation. These could be decisions related to product pricing, customer success or product development. These are the decisions that impact the growth of your company. Once you have done that, map out clearly the people involved in that decision. Use a roles-and-responsibilities framework like RACI (responsible, accountable, consulted and informed) to identify the one role/individual who ultimately has responsibility for making that decision. Then work with the leadership team to make that transparent across the organisation.

2. *Diversity, Equality and Inclusion Workout*
   Using data, look at the make-up of your organisation from a diversity, equality and inclusion perspective. What is the ratio of men to women in your leadership team, in management, in your organisation? Do this for under-represented minorities. With this data, clearly identify the actions you need to take as an organisation to make it more diverse. This plan will clearly map out where you need to develop more diverse talent internally and/or hire more diverse talent externally. This is an easy muscle to identify but a difficult one to develop. Your organisation will not continue to scale and grow unless you develop this muscle. This is a key workout!

3. *Hiring Practices Workout*

Have your HR or recruitment team map out the process for hiring people into the organisation. Ensure there is a clear job/role specification – what success in this role will look like. Ensure the people involved in the hiring process have been trained on what to look for in a person so that they can be successful in your organisation. Take a Goldilocks approach to the number of people involved in the hiring process – it should be more than three and less than seven.

4. *On-Boarding Process Workout*

Have someone on your leadership team map out the process for onboarding a new employee to the company. A clear 90-day plan should be put in place for each employee. They should have a clear plan on how to be fully contributing to their role in 90 days. If there is no plan in place, and they fail to be fully contributing to the company within 90 days, then this is the fault of the organisation, not the fault of the person. Be clear on expectations for the role, what success looks like in the role and who the key people are in the organisation to make them successful. Every employee should have a 90-day plan to onboard into the company culture, the company context and ultimately the company growth.

5. *Culture Language Workout*

Look at the last 10 presentations that were made to the executive leadership team by employees in the organisation. This could be the yearly planning process, the monthly sales figures update, customer feedback and the like. What words are used to describe success or failure in the organisation? Discuss with the leadership team whether you are comfortable that these are the words that are true to your organisational value, mission and vision. If not, then you need to start the process of inculcating the use of different words.

6. *Off-Boarding Process Workout*

Just as it is important to bring people on board the organisation in the right way, at some point you will need to let somebody go. Do you have a defined process to let people go? This is a symbiotic relationship with onboarding. Being clear on what success looks like in your organisation will help you communicate and message to people when the level of performance is not meeting expectations. Put in place a robust process to ensure you do this equitably, fairly and with respect for the person. Be clear on what role people are accountable for their performance, but be clear on what role the organisation plays here as well.

7. *'Acid Test of Culture' Workout*
    This is the easiest muscle to identify. If you have one of these in your organisation (or maybe you have more than one!) then you know exactly what this workout is. Act now on this person. If this person needs to stay (for reasons such as single point of failure, single key skill set), put in place a plan to modify the behaviour so they are not toxic to other employees in the organisation. Regardless of whether this will be successful or not, act now to mitigate the person leaving the organisation (through either voluntary or involuntary means). At some point sooner or later, either this person's behaviour needs to change or they need to leave. If action is not taken, they will become a roadblock to the organisation's plans for scaling and growing the company.

Are you now ready for the final workout?

7

Workout 7: Building a Growth Mindset – from Start-Up to Sustainable Growth

- To be open to feedback, both positive and constructive – to absorb the feedback
- To be receptive and resilient, to be experimental and adventurous
- To be focused on long-term growth

This final workout focuses on growth. For the organisation to grow and scale, every facet of the organisation must do exactly this – grow and scale.

Part 1: Discussion of the Organisational Muscle to Be Developed

The concept of the 'growth mindset' stems from research by the Stanford psychologist Dr Carole Dweck. In her research, Dr Dweck found that in the way we approach things, our 'mindset' can tend towards a 'fixed' mindset or a 'growth' mindset. The two approaches differ in how we as individuals view our abilities and capabilities and how we can learn to develop and enhance those capabilities. We can look at ability and capability as relatively fixed (we can work on improving some things but ultimately our capabilities are fixed in a certain way) or we can look at these issues from a growth perspective – with practice and lessons learned, we can learn to grow our abilities and capabilities.

For the purposes of this workout, we will look at the growth mindset as something that can be developed on individual, team-wide and organisational-wide levels.

An individual-level growth mindset approaches new opportunities, new challenges and new problems to be solved in a 'what can I learn from this' perspective. This translates into a viewpoint that 'I can solve this problem' and 'I can overcome this challenge'. There are two ways of doing this:

- I can solve this problem now because I have currently all the capabilities, resources and skills to do this now.
- I cannot solve this problem *yet*; however, with additional development through learning more about the problem and the skills, resources and capabilities I need to solve the problem, I will eventually be able to solve the problem. It is a matter of timing; I need to develop my skills further to do this. Additionally, I will look to any learning I acquire by not solving the problem at the first or second or nth attempt – and using this feedback and learning, I will solve the problem.

While not a universal phenomenon, most entrepreneurial leaders and founders who establish their own organisation will tend to adopt a growth mindset approach to how they do things. This is evident from both previous research and in the voices of the entrepreneurial leaders included in our research for this book. The workout challenge here is to ensure that the organisation (not just some individuals within the organisation, or even some of the teams) adopts a growth mindset throughout. As a leader, you want to grow and scale your organisation. Instilling a growth mindset into every individual in the organisation is a key part in making that happen!

Developing a growth mindset at an organisational level requires continual effort and practice. One of the key components of this is ensuring that the organisation has a strong emphasis on feedback and can create a context in which continual feedback is an integral part of how the organisation works.

This entrepreneurial leadership muscle is all about being willing to go out there and test the waters, – being open to feedback and being willing to adopt an individual leadership and organisational mindset involving moving from day-to-day survival to long-term organisational growth and sustainability – trying it out as you go along! Many start-up organisations may have a theory or a vision of how their product or service will work in the marketplace. They could approach the market with a fully baked product/service, having done extensive market research, or they might approach the market with a beta or test product that they will use to gain practical insight and feedback from customers in the market. Customer feedback can be negative – customers refuse to buy their product, or when they do buy it, they give negative feedback, either directly to the company or through review listings and websites. Conversely, feedback can be positive – consumers love and adopt the new product/service and give it great feedback.

The company can only know the actual consumer reaction to their start-up company by launching their product or service into the market. Regardless of which reaction the product or service receives, being open to the feedback from employees, stakeholders and customers is an important part of the organisational muscle to develop – and often one of the hardest. As the marketplace throws metaphorical punches at your start-up product and service, the organisation needs to develop the capability and the muscle to absorb the punches, while also reacting and adapting to the external landscape in which it is operating.

Thus, at an organisational level, there will be continual feedback from the market – from customers – on the product or service. The aim of this workout is to translate that external feedback internally into the organisation so that it drives actions and decisions that can help to further develop the product or service.

The organisation, however, is made up of people who individually and collectively must take ownership and accountability for accepting and using that feedback in such a way (using a growth mindset) that helps them to develop their own skills, capabilities and abilities. This continuous loop, incorporating feedback into decision-making and internal behaviour and actions, is an important muscle for the organisation to develop as it looks for long-term sustainable growth.

In the next section, we will hear some of the voices from entrepreneurial leaders gathered in our research and access their views on the need to have a growth mindset, and incorporating the feedback gained back into the organisation.

Part 2: Experiences of Entrepreneurial Leaders – Adopting a 'Growth' Mindset

Learning at the Start

> With young professionals, it's easier for the founders to communicate their ideas and the team makes it happen fast *they don't have a problem with obstacles*. But the reverse can happen too – it can be more difficult to get things going, if I want something to happen it takes longer,
> which can also be attributed to the company being still young; we are still testing at this stage, just like any other new company.

> It doesn't happen often that we reach a roadblock. We want to keep moving on; we might have an idea and we hit challenges, but in the end we adapt.

> We face challenges and sometimes it's tough, but I don't mind at all, that is how I have been able to learn. But I have found that if I have ideas in my head, I pursue them. I either find out that there is a better way to approach them or, if they fail, *I learn a lot and can try again*. It's a mindset issue – you go for it or you don't.

> If we come up with an idea, we want to execute it immediately. It may not always work, but *we like to try new things*; we are willing to put in the effort.

Sticking to the Vision – or Moving On

It could be that the founder's *original vision is working out,* but he is still struggling to realise the implications of it becoming a reality; he has a lot of challenges to overcome but is making the effort.

Every idea that is submitted is taking into account and discussed by the management team. We are happy to look at any ideas. *There's a lot of room for your own initiative* in the business, and we try to be positive about all possibilities.

I consider myself an innovator. I really like bringing ideas to life and it's actually part of the services I offer my clients – I want to help them with solutions that can make their business grow – this is part of making our business grow too.

Our founder's vision is working out, but he had to overcome a lot of obstacles. He is now more *successful in converting people to the vision* – both customers and staff members – but he had to give up on some of the old retainers who were never going to make a transition.

I have lots of ideas and I always want to test them. Normally I talk it over with my partners and we fine-tune it. There have been successes and failures, but I enjoy bringing them to life.

My vision was to create a small but value-adding unique consultancy especially geared to the local market and then keep it going … until I didn't want to do it anymore … I like the problem-solving work for my new clients the best, but am happy to work with those who just want to keep me on retainer – I see it all as *contributing to my personal growth.*

One of the reasons I managed to be successful at the beginning was because I made a point of going through with my ideas. Not always smoothly, but it is much worse to do nothing.

I think my vision worked out well. I have a nice business, it could be more – but I'm still working on it. I'm *quite restless about it.* I am willing to put in the effort to see it really take off. But I am happy to move on to the next idea.

Moving Away from the Original Plan

At the beginning my plan was a business on a much bigger scale, but now I realise that the high quality of my service is what differentiates me. It's a personal choice to keep the company small rather than getting it bigger. So, the plan for growth is limited.

We thought we knew where we were going, but where we are now
is not entirely the same – once we grew it was hard to pass the
same aims and objectives to everyone. We were growing so
fast; it was not so easy to explain the business idea and keep
pushing it.

My original vision was always my passion for some idea, then when
that dies – whether or not the company dies – it's time for
me to move on. This might be three to five years. If I want to
still be there then that's OK, but otherwise I'd rather get out.
I've been in this business now for two years. *It's not that I have
outgrown this job. Maybe it has outgrown me.*

I approach an issue with a certain methodology. I set my idea in
motion, and depending on the initial response or feedback, I
may change it according to the situation.

Hiring Growth-Mindset People

Lots of people working for us got incredible opportunities with us
… and that's what a lot of them loved about it. I remember two
or three people in their mid-20s being sent to set up a country
office from scratch and become country managers. And they
did it really well, coping with such a fast-growth environment,
having to work on their own.

I think it was a big part of the success, *hiring these young and
enthusiastic people.* I think what it did was it—it may have also
made for a lower cost base earlier on. It meant we probably got
more growth early on.

I found that as I started to recruit more experienced engineers
and more qualified people, they took the responsibility and it
became just so much easier to manage organisational growth,
and my *leadership style became more about communicating* and
working through the problem together, rather than telling
them what to do all the time.

I think it depends on how quickly the organisation is growing.
I think it happens relatively quickly, at different times, for
different leaders in the same organisation. As you build out
the business you will be changing leaders because they have
different skill sets – and for some of them, they
also like the job better when it's smaller, or for others, they
like it when it's bigger. You often don't know until you
hire them.

And it's a little bit of a timing issue: *When's the right time do to that
– hire more people?* This is a challenging decision for the
leadership team.

But It's Not Always So Easy

I think one of the problems with start-up businesses is that many start-up leaders normally recruit junior and inexperienced people – because *they're never brave enough to recruit expensive people* who've got ability and who can work with the leadership team at the same level. So the leaders are constantly having to nurture, advise and manage, and it is incredibly stressful.

Start-ups before they scale up can be much more non-hierarchical, and that actually causes problems for some of them later on as the companies grow. Sometimes the leaders can't let go of any little bit of it, but they do have to do this later. That's fine, you can do it when you've got 10 staff or 20, you can still do everything, but when it becomes 300, the chief executive cannot possibly know all the 300.

Moving On

When we went through our rapid growth phase, there was a family feeling around the business. Everyone together, working from 9 a.m. to 10 p.m. every day. That was the culture of that moment in time. *That family together was like a football team*, we were fighting together. That has changed a little now.

I think one of the things we both as co-founders got wrong with the company, we never realised how big it would become – and how we would manage this.

Nothing is set in stone; nothing can be guaranteed for long periods of time – or even short ones. There's just huge amount of fluidity in the environment in which we operate. We have to appreciate this lack of continuity and lack of predictability.

Crucially, given how a company typically scales up, the roles in the company have had to change very quickly. *We never properly defined the process to keep changing those roles.* At various points they were probably well defined; but six months later, the definition of the role had become ragged again.

It's the ability to think about what the future needs. So, what you have today with 25 people is different than what you're going to need with 100 people. So, what's the thing that you really have to have in place when you get to 100? And what's the thing down the road which is enough, fix it just a little bit, so it's okay at 100, and what's the stuff that you can completely ignore but it seems like you have to do something about? And I think the ability to make that decision, and to do that well, is what helps the company grow.

Thinking as a Growth-Mindset Leader

The best leaders I know never believe they're perfect, and they certainly never believe their own press. They're also open to feedback and frank criticism and they adjust accordingly. And whether you were born that way or whether you've learned over time, that's important.

Having the growth mindset, being super vocal and critical, *being able to recognise where your gaps are* and to fill them with people around you, and to be agile and continue that whole idea of continuous growth, has to have served people well … I think in some ways they can probably compensate around it, but then they also grow through their own experiences, right, and that luckily keeps pushing them to the next bigger scale and scope. Also, is this experiential leadership as a leader, and a form of leadership by your own experiences?

Definitely you evolve as a leader. And I think you have to adapt yourself to the people you bring in. You have to adapt yourself constantly. I think you should have your values and your style, but you really do have to be adaptable. *People work in very different styles.* Some people like working from home. Some people like working and being around people a lot of the time. Some people like face-to-face meetings. Some people like phone calls. Some people like other things. So long as the values are there, the values align with your organisation and who you are as an individual and who you want to bring in at the company, *you can adapt around the people and hopefully they will adapt around you, as well.*

Feedback Is King

I remember one of our very first employees, her saying to me, 'You totally don't understand how much your words mean to people … they're looking up to you way more than you realise.' And that was *when I learned more and more.*

Feedback – there are a lot of market forces here that will mask some deficits for a long time. As long as people are self-aware enough to round themselves out and change, I think they can get away with that.

What I'm seeing in the start-ups of today, the leaders in these organisations and in the scale-ups, is that they are much more open about asking for help. *They're much more collaborative and adaptable.*

Having that self-awareness, I think you could have experiences that will get you to kind of open up to that and realise that

others can grow and that you yourself can grow, but it takes
a certain level of self-awareness and the ability to be vocally
self-critical.

I think number one for entrepreneurial leadership survival
is being very self-aware. Through self-awareness you can
understand your weaknesses. My weakness, perhaps, I get
stressed out too quickly. If I get stressed out too quickly, how do
I combat that? I can do meditation, which I do by the way, twice
a day for twenty minutes. What else can I do? I can physically
exhaust myself in the gym. Great. Got myself a private trainer
and I work out in the gym. *It's constantly revaluating yourself.*

Being prepared to learn: – Things are never going to be perfect
and they're never going to work out the way you think they're
going to work out. You need to be constantly evolving what
your strategy and your plans are. And I think the degree to
which that is necessary has been a real tough learning curve
for me. Because it's not part of my natural make-up to be that
flexible, I tend to like structure and order and for things to be
moving according to a plan.

That concept of agility will be important just for the pace of
change and I don't see that slowing down any time soon. Your
ability to respond to change is going to always be important as
a leader.

Learning on the Job

It was an incredibly stressful period because I wasn't really set
up. I was almost doing everything myself and I found it really
hard. And I found it sort of difficult to ask people to do things
because I wasn't paying them much … So I found that really
difficult, to get through the transition, but when the company
started to get busy and too much had to happen it was really
the only way to try and drive the business forward. But I did
have quite a lot of challenges and really had to change.

In the first company that I started, *I made every mistake possible.*
When I listed them after I sold the first company, there were
48 mistakes, right? Now once you have all those mistakes,
you decide what you want to do about it. You could give up.
You say, 'Oh, I'm just the world's worst leader. I should never
start another company, or I should not even take a leadership
position.'

I learned, by having so many failed projects, that there's no point
dwelling on something for too long. With the feedback you're
getting and if you don't think it's going to work, the best way
to find out is through rapid experimentation – if that's talking

to people or if that's doing something online, whether it be a survey or whether it be, I don't know, Google ads or something. People are honest. They generally, actually, don't really skirt around things that you're saying, unless it's maybe a relative or close friend trying to be polite.

Adapt and change: Being able *to relate to people at all levels* is something that I think the entrepreneurial leaders today really have, which entrepreneurs of yesterday didn't.

You need to know your industry inside out nowadays ... keeping up with what's going on. That can lead to burnout if you don't have a mindset of 'how do I compartmentalise things?' By the way, there's also a compartment that's labelled 'me, my health, my family, my holidays', all of that.

Part 3: Organisational Muscle Workout Practice – Moving from the Current State to the Future State

- Understand the current and necessary future state of this organisational muscle.
- Through this identify the organisational muscle to be developed.
- Put in place a workout plan to develop the muscle – with milestones, targets and regular check-ins on whether the muscle is being developed.

These are the seven key questions to ask yourself to diagnose the current state of your organisational 'growth mindset' muscle:

1. Hiring: As you hire people into the organisation, do you look for a 'growth mindset' from potential candidates? What questions do you use to help understand and assess a candidate's growth-mindset approach? How do you assess whether they will be successful in supporting the organisation to grow and scale?
2. Customer feedback: What processes and mechanisms do you have in place to gain feedback from the customer? Who is responsible in the organisation for analysing and understanding each piece of customer feedback? How do you systemically incorporate customer feedback into the organisation?

3. Internal feedback culture: How open are you as a leadership team to receive feedback from employees? How do you communicate to employees – is this communication process two-way and dynamic or just one-way? Is there a weekly or monthly 'all-hands' meeting where you allow open questions and answers from employees? Do you as a leadership team actively solicit feedback from employees on yourself? How do you do this? Is there a process internally for employees to give anonymous feedback and suggestions? Do you as a leadership team actively promote feedback and suggestions through a variety of mechanisms in the organisation?

4. Pre- and post-mortem: Do you employ the concept of 'pre-' and 'post-'mortems in your organisation as a way of understanding the likely success of a project or process? Do you then conduct a post-review to understand what went well and what did not go so well? How do you incorporate those data points into your organisation – pre-mortem (before the event) and post-mortem (after the event)?

5. Processes: When was the last time you looked at your 10 key internal processes? Are they still fit for purpose? Have they adapted and evolved as the organisation has adapted and evolved? Are these processes clearly understood by everyone in the organisation? Are the processes documented, or are they inside one employee's head?

6. Surveys: The adage states that what gets measured gets done in an organisation. What are your measures of success internal to the organisation? What mechanism do you use to measure this success? How often do you conduct formal surveys in your organisation – from employee engagement surveys to process surveys? Is there a survey strategy in the organisation to support continual data points and feedback from the organisation?

7. Skip-level meetings: How often do leaders and managers in the organisation meet with employees one or two levels below them in the organisation? Do you, as an executive leadership team, exercise the muscle of spending time deeper in the organisation to understand the concerns at this level in the organisation – what is working well, what is not working so well?

Having asked yourself and the leadership team these questions and answered them honestly, what is your workout plan to help you get from your current state of organisational muscle to your future state? Below are some workouts to help you achieve those plans.

Workout Plan

1. *Hiring People Workout*

    Put in place a formal part of your recruitment process that assesses the 'growth mindset' of potential employees. Identify the top 10 people in your organisation with this growth mindset and make them part of the hiring process. Their role should be to assess this capability in potential candidates. Ask potential employees the question, 'Tell me about a time that you didn't succeed at something.' Look for what they learned, how they adapted and how this helped them to grow and develop.

2. *Customer Feedback Workout*

    If you do not have one already, put in place a customer success leader in your organisation. The aim is to make customers successful – as this will make the company successful. Ensure this person and their team are in constant contact with customers – through either surveys, customer roundtables or briefings – and involve customers in pilots with your product or service. Put in place a process for this team to incorporate customer feedback into the organisation to provide a robust way of improving internal processes, procedures and, ultimately, the product or service being offered to the customer.

3. *Internal Feedback Culture Workout*

    Ensure every employee in your organisation has feedback training. This training should give them the framework to give feedback and how to take feedback. It also provides a clear signal to the organisation, that constant feedback is an important muscle to continually focus on and develop. Start every interaction with employees with a question: 'Have you any feedback for me – is there anything that either I, the leadership team or the organisation should continue to do, stop doing or start to do?' Using this question internally in your organisation will role-model a feedback culture and will elicit an enormous amount of data to help you continue to grow and develop your organisation. It sets the tone for scaling a growth mindset in the organisation.

4. *Pre- and Post-mortems Workout*
    For every new process, new project, new product or service launch, have the team do both a pre- and a post-mortem. A pre-mortem is a list of things that the team feels is likely to happen – both positive and not so positive things – before the new process, project or product is launched. This process can also help the team determine the definition of success for the new project or product. Doing this also helps to get ahead of potential issues with a new product or service. After it has launched, conduct a post-mortem with the team – what went well that you should continue to do, what did not go so well that you should stop or do better, what things you did not do this time that you should incorporate into the next project, product or service? Continually doing this will flex and build your organisational growth-mindset muscle.

5. *Building Processes Workout*
    As you scale the company, processes will continually break and fail. This is an incredibly positive part of growing and scaling your company. Processes built for handling 100 customers likely will not suffice for 10,000 customers. Identify your top 10 processes in the organisation. Review these processes on a regular basis to ensure they are fit for purpose. Ideally, build some element of 'future-proofing' into your most important processes. That way they can last longer and do not need to be reviewed as often.

6. *Monitoring and Surveying Workout*
    Continually survey your organisation, both internally and externally, to get an up-to-date pulse check on what is happening in the company. Regular employee surveys (e.g. quarterly) give you a quick update on what is working well in the organisation, which programmes are having a positive impact and which are not have the desired impact. Use engagement surveys to understand how employees are feeling about the organisation and their role in the organisation. Use hiring surveys to understand how well the organisation is meeting the needs and expectations of new employees (this can be

a significant predictor of employee turnover in the organisation). Use attrition surveys to understand why people are leaving. Using the data gleaned from these surveys can help the organisation predict likely outcomes (who might leave the organisation) as well as allow it to put in place programmes to address employee concerns.

7.   *Skip-Level Meetings Workout*

Formalise 'skip-level' meetings in the organisation. Each leader and manager should meet either 1:1 or in a small team with employees, at least one level below them in the company hierarchy. Do this on a regular basis (at least quarterly or, better still, monthly). This will allow leaders and managers to gather feedback from deeper in the organisation to allow them to understand what is happening across the company. Doing this regularly also demonstrates the organisation's commitment to continually getting feedback. The meetings should be open, and the purpose is to give employees who might not ordinarily have direct access to a senior leader the opportunity to gain access and give feedback.

By focusing on these seven key workouts, the organisation will continually identify and develop the organisational muscle to embed a growth mindset. This will empower the organisation to adopt a mindset and an approach that will help to grow and develop.

8

Bringing the Workouts to Life

Over the last seven chapters, through our research, we have introduced you to seven key workouts that we see as essential to developing entrepreneurial leadership organisational muscles in your company. We have explored each of the muscles in detail, we have used the voices and experiences of the entrepreneurial leaders to whom we have spoken in our research to reinforce our understanding of the importance of developing these muscles, and we have noted the key challenges associated with identifying and building these vital organisational muscles. Through asking a series of focused questions, we have explored these seven key workouts, designed to grow this organisational capability.

For this last chapter in the book, our aim is to bring 'alive' some of these workouts, with specific examples of entrepreneurial leaders and their teams who have displayed and developed these organisational muscles in action.

Workout 1: Letting Go of Autonomy

A good example of demonstrating the ability to let go of autonomy is Tom Blomfield, the founder of start-up bank Monzo, founded in 2015. One of Britain's first digital-only banks, Blomfield managed to grow Monzo into one of the most successful banks of its kind in recent years, gaining almost five million customers in a short time. In an interview with TechCrunch, Blomfield (2021) revealed that he started struggling with health issues, related to the pandemic, and therefore decided to hand over his role of chief executive and move into the newly created role of president. His decision to step down means he has left day-to-day operations at the bank, but he will retain a stake in the business. It illustrates Blomfield's ability to let go of a need for autonomy, thereby trying to help the business move forward. Along with this, Blomfield has illustrated a balance in his capabilities by arguably demonstrating the workouts of anticipating future problems (founding one of Britain's first completely digital banks) and allowing for role evolution (creating the new role of president). Blomfield therefore illustrates the advantage that a good balance of workouts can create.

A significant motivator for entrepreneurial leaders to start up their own business is the value they place on their autonomy. The ironic challenge faced by some founders and leaders in start-ups is that letting go of this precious autonomy is an important aspect in the scaling-up phase of a business. It can be suggested that the essence of letting go of autonomy lies in the fact that more problems need to be dealt with as the business grows. It becomes simply impossible to keep making every decision alone at the top, and therefore it is of crucial essence to start distributing autonomy across the company.

Sometimes this need for autonomy and the 'I'll do it all by myself' notion is so engrained in the behaviour of many entrepreneurial leaders that they often forget the strengths and talents of their teams, and the value that delegation can add to their business. As Reid Hoffman, co-founder of Linked-In, argued, 'No matter how brilliant your mind or strategy, if you're playing a solo game, you'll always lose out to a team.' Indeed, stubborn leaders who refuse to step down when necessary often finds themselves being forced out by investors. Anecdotal evidence suggests that as many as three-quarters of start-up CEOs are fired after a succession of funding rounds on the way to scale-up.

Losing the obsession with autonomy and improving delegation can also speed things up and free up the leadership team to be more strategic. As explained in a McKinsey article (De Smet, Gagnon and Mygatt, 2021), 'organizations that make decisions quickly are twice as likely as slow decision-makers to make high-quality decisions. Organizations that consistently decide fast and well are, in turn, more likely to outperform their peers.'

This usually means increasingly allocating decision-making to executives, teams and individuals within the organisation. This then gives the top teams the time to focus on the core business decisions. An example of an entrepreneur who has established this kind of devolved decision-making structure in his organisation is Jack Ma, co-founder of Alibaba. As also suggested by the same McKinsey article, most of Alibaba's operating decisions are made by small teams informed by machine learning and creative applications of data. The company's C-level executives focus on cross-cutting decisions, including resource allocation for top initiatives. This allows the company to make decisions quickly, cutting time on decisions and processes through reducing by half the number of steps which most executives imagine are necessary. This kind of streamlining is vital to increasing decision speed and gives Alibaba a major competitive edge.

Workout 2: Anticipating Future Problems

An interesting example of the ability of an entrepreneurial leader to 'anticipate the future' is the current CEO of Tesla, Elon Musk. Musk has demonstrated his ability to anticipate future problems not once but several times by setting up multiple successful businesses like Tesla or SpaceX. The changes in the car market towards electric vehicles has been around for some time, but it is Musk (through Tesla) who has turbocharged the evolution of cars from fossil fuels to electric. And for some, that is just the beginning of the revolution. 'Tesla's mission is not to sell cars, or even to sell batteries, it goes much further. Its mission is to anticipate the future, a much better future, and to make it easier for us to think about how to get there' (Dans, 2019). This anticipation of future problems is so valued by the market that at the time of writing (March 2021), Tesla's value, as measured by market capitalisation, is more than the combined value of the other nine largest carmakers in the world.

Another good example is the videoconferencing (and more!) software company Zoom, under the leadership of CEO Eric Yuan. Anticipating the shift to digitalisation under an increasingly international world, Zoom began facilitating video calls back in 2012. Known for its universal compatibility and simple, user-friendly design, Zoom's success skyrocketed in 2020 and the word 'Zoom' has now become synonymous with 'video call'. In an article about Zoom's success over the past year, Cashen (2020) praises founder Yuan's dedication to 'making customer satisfaction and happiness a priority', explaining that his success has been a long time coming. Speaking of the inspiration for the company and showing his impressive anticipation of the future, Yuan explained how the idea came to him on 10-hour-long train journeys to visit his girlfriend – how he wished he had some way of seeing her on a smart device with just a few clicks. The inclusion of 'Zoom' in the *Oxford English Dictionary* in late 2020 as a verb – defined as 'to communicate with somebody over the internet, typically by video chat, using the software application Zoom' – is arguably a clear indication of a sustainable business having anticipated future workplace needs!

Workout 3: Changing Your Focus from Being Customer-Driven to Problem-Solving 360°.

Probably the poster child of customer focus over the past 20 years has been Amazon, with their obsession with the customer and a maniacal culture of focus on customer satisfaction. However, this is only part of the story. Their operational, functioning internal structure is focused on problem-solving 360°. Beth Galetti (2020), senior vice president of human resources at Amazon, argued in a McKinsey article that the pace of change requires companies to continually learn and adapt, a reality which has led Amazon to cultivate a culture of continuous learning and put in place the infrastructure to support it. Jeff Bezos and his leadership team neatly encapsulate this focus on problem-solving 360° by regularly declaring that it is 'Still Day One' in their business, and using this as a vital element of their culture.

Another classic example of evolving a company focus from being customer-driven to problem-solving is Apple, specifically Steve Jobs's approach. Whilst the popular phrase often referred to when discussing entrepreneurship and business is 'The customer is always right', Jobs felt that the exact opposite was true. He once explained, 'Some people say give the customers what they want, but that's not my approach. Our job is to figure out what they're going to want before they do.' Taking this (at the time) unconventional approach, Jobs did exactly what he said he would do, and gave the public revolutionary technology products that they definitely did not realise they needed – but on which they soon became dependent.

Amazon's growth story from a start-up in Seattle in 1996 to the absolute behemoth that it is today (it can be said that it has scaled up indeed) is due largely in part to its evolution from just being customer-focused to solving customer problems, before they even know there is a problem – as in Apple's case, above.

Workout 4: Allowing for Role Evolution

One of the most high-profile examples of this organisational muscle being identified, grown and developed in recent times is Google's hiring of Eric Schmidt as CEO in 2001. By 2001, as Google continued to grow and scale, Google's Board (and its two founders Larry Page and Sergey Brin) recognised that the company (and by definition Page and Brin themselves) did not have the capabilities in place in order to continue to grow and scale the organisation. Therefore, the organisational roles needed to evolve, and more talent had to be brought into the organisation on the executive team. Schmidt's CEO role focused on the management of the vice presidents and the sales organisation (areas where Page and Brin had little experience). Additionally, Schmidt's job responsibilities included building the corporate infrastructure needed to maintain Google's rapid growth as a company. Having done the job which he was hired to do, and having brought the additional organisational muscle to the company, Schmidt worked closely with Page and Brin, to arguably enable Page to once again become CEO of Google, and Schmidt was elevated to the role of executive chairman, in a clear example of allowing for role evolution.

Workout 5: Coping with Risk

In 2017, Dara Khosrowshahi became the CEO of Uber. With a large market share at the time and clear potential for growth of this novel business, there were significant risks both with the business and with Khosrowshahi taking on the role. One of the risks, as a

Forbes article described at the time, was that Uber 'continues to lose hundreds of millions of dollars each quarter. The company has also lost several top executives in recent months, including its chief financial and chief operating officers, and faces a critical legal challenge from Google spin-off Waymo, which accused Uber of stealing its intellectual property' (Helft, 2018). These represented a considerable in-tray of challenges for an incoming CEO, but Khosrowshahi's ability to cope with risk as a leader showed in taking on the job as CEO at this time.

Spending three years untangling all the risks that he had inherited, in 2020 Uber's CEO was faced with the entire business model being put under pressure with the lockdowns enforced in several of its key markets due to the Covid-19 pandemic. Bookings on its hail-riding service plummeted and were down up to 80 per cent at one point. Khosrowshahi and his leadership team managed to take advantage of the huge growth in the food delivery sector, and nimbly shifted resources and focus to 'Uber Eats'. The rapid 89 per cent growth in Uber Eats bookings immediately took some of the pain from the huge decrease in customer ride bookings.

While the jury is still somehow out on the long-term profitability of Uber (it still lost over $1 billion dollars in Q3 2020), given the risks that the Khosrowshahi took on when he assumed the role in 2017 and given the business risks that the Covid-19 pandemic had thrown up for the business model of Uber, arguably he and his leadership team have demonstrated a strong capacity and capability not only to cope with risk but also to thrive from it.

Workout 6: Managing Cultural Change

Jim Bilefield is a serial digital entrepreneur who has been involved in a number of technology-focused start-up organisations. Part of the founding leadership team of Skype as well as an investor in several other start-up companies around the globe, Bilefield has a strong understanding of the development of organisational muscle in managing culture change in organisations. When asked about the role culture plays in Skype's business (Bilefield, 2020), he remarked,

A strong, positive culture is critical to enable a rapid and healthy scale-up. We made sure at Skype that we carried our unique culture with us around the world, though it evolved as we both grew up and entered new geographies and learned that what works in Tallinn may not necessarily work in Los Angeles. Yet some of the fundamental tenets of Skype's culture, inculcated in all early employees by the Scandinavian founders and lead Estonian engineers, remained clear: global in mindset, revolutionary in ambition, distrustful of hierarchy, and customer obsessed.

Managing cultural change is an important muscle to develop because of the constant changes and expansion that can come along while scaling up the business. Bilefield is clear that having this organisational muscle developed in an organisation is crucial to scaling up the business for the long term.

Workout 7: Building a Growth Mindset

MovementX is a US-based company that provides one-on-one, hands-on physical therapy. Like many organisations, particularly those whose business model was predicated on in-person customer interaction, the Covid-19 pandemic has had a dramatic impact on this business model, and the organisation had to lean heavily on their organisational growth-mindset muscle to cope with the rapid rate of change. As co-founder Dr Fred Gilbert (2021) told Forbes in an article, 'The initial impact of the Covid-19 pandemic and shutdown was a dramatic drop in business as our patients and providers got their bearings around the situation. To survive, MovementX knew we had to prioritize finding alternative ways to provide high-quality and safe care in this new environment.' And that is exactly what they did by shifting the business model primarily to telehealth, with some in-person socially distanced sessions. MovementX launched an online virtual exercise series designed for the population most affected by the pandemic – older adults – while recognising the important role of physical therapy in keeping the pandemic-impacted society moving both physically and mentally. So, the company activated the growth-mindset muscle in their organisation to alleviate the impact the pandemic was having on its business model and customer base, continually innovating during this crisis. As an outcome of this enforced switch in the way of operating, the company experienced a dramatic increase in the number of applications from therapists to join their organisation and avail themselves of this new business model, enabling MovementX to significantly grow their turnover and service offerings. Flexing and utilising their organisational leadership growth-mindset muscle has had a direct impact on helping the business scale up during the challenges of the early 2020s.

Conclusion: Keeping in Shape: An Ongoing Process

For your entrepreneurial leadership team to keep in shape, to keep exercising those muscles, to keep doing the workouts, to be among the start-ups to successfully 'scale up' to become the next Slack, Zoom or Uber – to be among the one per cent of the start-ups who make it to the big time – you have to keep at it. Like all gymnasts and sportspeople know, if you start taking it easy and miss those gym appointments, those muscles you worked so hard to build will soon turn to flab.

So you have been building the muscle power to succeed. You can now talent-spot entrepreneurial muscle power – it takes one to know one. You are now able to convince others (having started with yourself and your family) that you can survive and thrive in a competitive world and have the muscle to make it happen.

It all depends on whether or not you have this very special *entrepreneurial leadership muscle* – and/or if you can see it in others. As an entrepreneur, the most important challenge for you is to be able to identify, develop, build and use this necessary muscle to make things happen in a sustainable way. Doing the workouts here will help you to get there. As an investor, you have been looking for the readable signs of muscle power amongst the entrepreneurial leaders passing your radar screens. You are now in better shape to screen in and screen out talent. But you need to keep alert. Use it or lose it!

Many of the examples we have quoted here are recently established high-growth organisations, bringing new and innovative products to market at an extremely rapid pace. In a relatively short organisational life span they have grown into multibillion-dollar organisations very rapidly. They have something that the others don't – entrepreneurial leadership muscle – and have built it up and are now focused on keeping it up.

In the series of workouts/exercises for leaders and their teams described in this book, we have explored the need to develop fitness for purpose in the start-up to scale-up process. This has involved building strength, endurance, agility, leanness, flexibility, suppleness, an ability to cope with adversity, and resilience. These have been geared towards scaling up transitional business ideas from start-up to long-term sustainability. We have also aimed these workouts to be relevant to organisations that are having to revisit or rework their established business models to adapt their businesses to the extreme volatility that is currently reshaping the business landscape.

Keeping in Shape with the Seven 'Developing Leadership Muscle' Workouts

As a start-up leader with a team hell-bent on scaling up the business, you have been focused on developing more organisational muscle, based on identifying and building up the gaps in your own and the team's muscle power to achieve the immediate organisational objectives. You have also been working on building up the overall muscle strength of the company and ensuring its resilience for the future. In the process of practising each of these workouts, you have been focused on specific muscle groups and adding additional organisational muscle power in order to move from your current to a future state. And you mustn't stop!

Adding organisational muscle can be a combination of further developing the strengths and power you have internally in the business, and bringing more capability into the current business through recruiting strongmen (and strongwomen) into the team.

Through these workouts – some you can do easily and some you just can't, try as you might – you have hopefully achieved the balance – of building on those internal strengths and bringing in additional organisational capability from the outside to augment the current organisational prowess and muscle set. All the best sports teams do it: grow their own, and at the same time bring in the 'mercenaries' – the job-hopping talent that adds a lot of value and then moves on. Catch them whilst you can.

The series of workouts or lessons described here – to enable you to practise for yourself and apply as an organisation – have been designed to help a start-up move to a more scaled-up operation capable of sustainable business growth, or to enable the leadership team to rethink and revisit their current business models to be in good shape for the future, especially in times of increasing uncertainty.

The Seven Workouts – One by One

Workout 1: Letting Go of Autonomy – from Founder-Led to Team Leadership – and Beyond

It's not easy for the leadership team to keep delegating, trusting and devolving decision-making when they actually really want to keep it all for themselves. There's a temptation to grab it all back at any point and go back to square one, especially if a new recruit given a lot of responsibility goes off and makes a major blunder. But that's the way that he or she learns. Letting go is never easy (especially for founders), and it's a big stretch for them to see others moving into 'their' C-suite. But it's the only way to achieve real growth and sustainability, and to keep sanity and resilience and energy. Otherwise all that muscle power gets sucked up in the day-to-day and is not exercised in preparing for the future workouts, and building strength in other body areas. To be really fit, it's no good just focusing on one set of muscles. The whole body must be toned and ready.

Workout 2: Anticipating Future Problems – from Solving One at a Time to Coping with Many –– from the Here and Now to the Future

In the early days of the start-up, the founders tend to be mostly reactive, living and managing from day to day, hoping that there will be a long-term future but never too sure about this. So when business turns up they will be working on it straight away. Immediate problems must be solved immediately. So working on the muscle of letting go of an obsession of reacting to problems as they emerge in real time to actually doing more blue-sky dreaming – and thinking about the future and getting ready for it – can be hard. And there is a tendency to abandon Workout 2 with the thought that maybe this one's for later, when the start-up is more established. But it never will be established until there's a mindset shift towards pro-activity, the use of continuous improvement, initiative, openness to new ideas and challenging the status quo – this muscle needs to be worked out regularly, right from the start.

Workout 3: Changing Your Focus –from Being Customer-Driven to Problem-Solving 360° – from Looking Outside to Looking Inside

When the business is first set up, most entrepreneurial leaders/ founders are busy with their customers – serving their needs was the impetus to start up from the beginning. And the work for these first customers pays the bills and helps the business to continue day by day. But this kind of exclusive focus can keep the business small. Many founder teams think they must wait until there are more and more customers with more and more business before they even think about increasing and then managing organisational capability – but this should not be left too late. The 'thinking about organisational resources' muscle is needed sooner rather than later. The narrow focus must be widened – and from the start. Founders who dream big can and will grow – if that muscle set can be worked on and expanded. The 'looking after customers' muscle will be used every day and might be suffering from overstrain. And the 'looking to the inside' muscle – often neglected – is a vital enabling muscle which will take up more and more time to grow, unless it's exercised from the start.

Workout 4: Allowing for Role Evolution – from Lack of Role Clarity to Role Definition

At the beginning of the entrepreneurial venture, the team does whatever is needed, when it's needed, without a thought of job descriptions and position specifications. Many such founders deliberately avoid these, especially as escaping from bureaucracy was always one of the plans in starting up the business. But there is a tendency for start-up leaders to just do the jobs they like. That's why they started the businesses – to do what they like. But this is rarely possible, realistically.

Businesses scaling up need to exercise the 'changing goals and tasks' muscle, building flexibility in not just being able to adopt different roles but wanting to take them on, and anticipating needs in directing teams for the future and in navigating more and more complexity. Scaled-up businesses need clarity on who does what. It doesn't matter when everyone mucks in during the start-up phase. However, as the business grows, that bureaucracy inevitably creeps in, but it doesn't have to be seen negatively. Building the role-definition muscle is needed, but still in balance with the other muscle groups.

Workout 5: Coping with Risk – from One Single Point of Failure to Juggling Several Products, Processes and People Issues – Understanding Systemic Risk

Start-up businesses fail often and easily, and their founders use their resilience muscles to just start up again, but to be sustainable the 'ability to cope with multiple risks' muscle must be worked on. As businesses grow, they not only get more complex but can also get more risky, and the nature of the risk changes. But the endless-analysis muscle mustn't be overused here, otherwise time will stand still. The 'cope with and minimise risk' muscle needs to be regularly developed, as well as the 'seeing the big picture despite the risk' muscle.

A useful muscle which some founders develop more than others is the 'implications down the line' muscle – thinking through new possibilities, weighing up the pros and cons, but not letting the cons stop the new ideas from flowing. Managing systemic and interrelated risks – balancing the house of cards – is very scary, but courage is a key nutrient for those exercising the building of entrepreneurial leadership muscles.

Workout 6: Managing Culture Change – Understanding Person–Culture Fit from an Additive Start-Up to Matching the Values of a Sustainable Business

Founding leadership teams don't often think about the culture of their organisation – it's just there. And when they hire new people, they are often consciously or subconsciously using their culture-fit muscle – which some leaders have already instinctively developed. But are they clear about what is the real culture – and is this what they want it to be, or something else? The workout to identify cultural norms can be very helpful here, especially if exercised regularly. But the start-up can't be too inward-looking – it will soon need to develop the culture-additive muscle, to absorb and make the best of new and evolving subcultures in the developing organisation. It can be easy to reject new cultures if this muscle isn't there, and that won't help the business to grow. The 'constructive absorption of new muscles' culture is needed in an ongoing way. The organisational muscle as a whole can be strengthened, not diluted, with the cooperation between cultures, all adding their own value to different parts of the body.

Workout 7: Building a Growth Mindset – from Start-Up to Sustainable Growth

Start-up leaders very often have a highly developed growth-mindset muscle from the beginning, but this muscle can get neglected when other muscles are used more in the early days – the tendency to immediately resolve customer issues, the ongoing focus on keep autonomy, working in the here and now, the mixing of roles, the worry about failure, and sometimes the mono-culture growth focus. The growth-mindset muscle has to be exercised in a conscious way despite many distractions to work out other muscles to give immediate strength and muscle power. The 'openness to feedback' muscle can get ignored in the rapid pace of development, but the process of receiving and accepting criticism can avoid problems later. The growth-mindset elements of being adventurous, resilient and experimental are muscles which still need regular attention, even as the entrepreneurial leadership team hardly has time to go to the gym anymore. Neglect these and fail to scale up!

Keeping in Shape – Ongoing Muscle-Building

Use the seven workouts as a way of analysing where you are now on the start-up to scaled-up trajectory: Which muscle groups are well developed? Frequently exercised? Looking strong? Which are still underused, or even overused? How dangerous is this? Are the founders still clinging on to a need for autonomy? Are they still mostly in the here and now, worrying where the cash for the salaries will come from? Are the founders still avoiding planning for an organisational structure and hoping it will just emerge? Are they still all doing every job that needs doing? Are they able to cope with managing multiple, coexisting risks? Has the business moved to being culture-additive? This in particular can be a litmus test of the point of achievement on the start-up to scaled-up voyage. And finally, are the growth mindsets still there? Or has this muscle atrophied?

Read the experiences of the entrepreneurial leaders in each workout chapter. Do you sound like you are on top of that workout goal? Or hesitating to jump on the treadmill or pick up those particular dumbbells? Getting started, investing in that gym membership, putting on the training shoes – then following the workout regimes – it's not easy and, like all resolutions, often gets forgotten. But building the seven entrepreneurial leadership muscles – according to the dozens of scaled-up leaders all over the world interviewed for this book – is the way forward to break out of the always-a-start-up trap. Go for it!

References

Bilefield, J. (2020, April 13). Interview (McKinsey). Retrieved from: https://www.mckinsey.com/business-functions/mckinsey-digital/our-insights/what-start-ups-need-to-scale-and-succeed.

Blomfield, T. (2021, January 20). Interview (TechCrunch). Retrieved from: https://techcrunch.com/2021/01/20/enjoying-life-again/.

Buffet, W. (2020, February 24). 'Buffett: Coronavirus Threat Shouldn't Change How You Invest' [video file]. Retrieved from: https://buffett.cnbc.com/video/2020/02/25/buffett-coronavirus-threat-shouldnt-change-how-you-invest.html.

Cashen, E. (2020). 'The Zoom Boom'. Retrieved from: https://www.worldfinance.com/special-reports/the-zoom-boom.

Dans, E. (2019). 'The Secret of Tesla's Success Is Not Selling Cars: It's Being Able to Anticipate the Future'. Retrieved from: https://www.forbes.com/sites/enriquedans/2019/09/09/the-secret-of-teslas-success-is-not-selling-cars-its-being-able-to-anticipate-thefuture/?sh=6842dbd04973.

De Smet, A., Gagnon, C., and Mygatt, E. (2021, January 11). 'Organizing for the Future: Nine Keys to Becoming a Future-Ready Company'. Retrieved from: https://www.mckinsey.com/business-functions/organization/our-insights/organizing-for-the-future-nine-keys-to-becoming-a-future-ready-company.

Dweck, Carol (2006). *Mindset: The New Psychology of Success*. New York: Ballantine Books.

Fernandes, T. (2014, August 1). Interview (McKinsey). Retrieved from: https://www.mckinsey.com/industries/public-and-social-sector/our-insights/tony-fernandes-on-driving-asean-entrepreneurship.

Forbes (2021, February 18). 'How to Build a Resilient Organization for a Post-Pandemic World'. Retrieved from: https://www.forbes.com/sites/deloitte/2021/02/18/how-to-build-a-resilient-organization-for-a-post-pandemic-world/?sh=3a00b84133f3.

Galetti, B. (2020, February 18). Interview (McKinsey). Retrieved from: https://www.mckinsey.com/business-functions/mckinsey-digital/our-insights/fasttimes/interviews/beth-galetti.

Georgadze, T. (2020, July 10). Interview (McKinsey). Retrieved from: https://www.mckinsey.com/business-functions/mckinsey-digital/our-insights/when-start-ups-scale-up-lessons-on-building-up-culture-and-talent.

Gilbert, F. (2021, May 21). Interview (Forbes). Retrieved from: https://www.forbes.com/sites/maryabbajay/2020/05/21/3-inspiring-small-business-stories-on-how-to-survive-during-covid-19/?sh=34bfc4074173.

Graham, P. (2021, February 12). Interview (Forbes). Retrieved from: https://www.forbes.com/sites/abdoriani/2021/02/12/insights-about-startup-hiring-in-the-early-versus-growth-stages/?ss=leadership-strategy&sh=7631a0076861.

Halla, N. (2020, August 12). Interview (McKinsey). Retrieved from: https://www.mckinsey.com/business-functions/mckinsey-digital/our-insights/scaling-a-start-up-launching-innovative-products-in-international-markets.

Helft, M. (2018). 'Uber Selects Expedia's Dara Khosrowshahi as Its New CEO'. Retrieved from: https://www.forbes.com/sites/miguelhelft/2017/08/27/uber-names-expedias-dara-khosrowshahi-as-its-new-ceo/?sh=13b1cb8d267e.

Huerta Hernandez, Claudia (2020). 'The Influence of National Cultural Background on Entrepreneurial Leadership Practice – Examples from Six Countries'. MBA thesis, Maastricht School of Management.

Krogerus, Mikael, and Tschappeler, Roman (2008). *The Decision Book*. London: Profile Books.

Lindinger, M. (2021, February 18). 'Five Ways to Be a Successful Remote Leader'. Retrieved from: https://www.forbes.com/sites/forbescoachescouncil/2021/02/18/five-ways-to-be-a-successful-remote-leader/?sh=1a2c1a0d50d.

Porterfield, C. (2019, December 24). 'Uber Cofounder Travis Kalanick to Resign from Board'. Retrieved from: https://www.forbes.com/sites/carlieporterfield/2019/12/24/uber-co-founder-travis-kalanick-to-resign-from-board/?sh=60c5ecc470f6.

Tynan, Martin (2020). 'Leading the Journey from Start-Up to Scaled-Up Organisations: The Evolution of Entrepreneurial Leadership Practice during Organisational Growth in Technology-Focused Organisations: A Roadmap for Stakeholders'. DBA thesis, Maastricht School of Management.

Lightning Source UK Ltd.
Milton Keynes UK
UKHW041251041221
394876UK00005B/88